UNCHOSEN

THE TRUTH ABOUT CALVINISM AND WHAT IT MEANS FOR THE WORLD

TYLER MILLER

Unchosen
Copyright © 2017 by Tyler Miller
All rights reserved.

To contact the author about speaking at your church or conference,
please go to www.upperroomyork.com or Isaiah403.org

All Scripture quotations, unless otherwise indicated, are taken from the New King James Version®. Copyright © 1982 by Thomas Nelson, Inc. Used by permission. All rights reserved.

Cover photo by Ian Espinosa
www.unsplash.com

ISBN-13: 978-1979382038
ISBN-10: 1979382034

To my amazing wife, who has stood with me every step of the way
and encouraged me to publish this book.

To my faithful brothers of the Upper Room who have provoked me
to early morning prayer, a passion for souls,
and a love for the truth.

CONTENTS

PREFACE

INTRODUCTION – *The basic difference between Calvinism and Arminianism*

CHAPTER 1: TULIP – *An overview of Calvinism's Five Points*

CHAPTER 2: DEPRAVITY – *How severe is our sin and depravity?*

CHAPTER 3: REGENERATION – *Are we born again before we repent and believe?*

CHAPTER 4: ELECTION – *Does the Bible defend predestination?*

CHAPTER 5: PROVIDENCE – *Is God behind everything that happens in the world?*

CHAPTER 6: ATONEMENT - *Who exactly did Jesus die for?*

CHAPTER 7: GRACE – *Is God's grace an undeserved favor or an irresistible force?*

CHAPTER 8: FAITH - *Does our faith matter to God and influence His will?*

CHAPTER 9: PERSEVERANCE – *Is Eternal Security an unconditional guarantee?*

CONCLUSION - *Ten extra reasons to reject Calvinism*

PREFACE

Many years ago I heard a powerful sermon on the Gospel of Jesus Christ. Though I had gone to Church my whole life, somehow I had taken this glorious, fundamental truth of Christianity for granted. But now, in one compelling sermon, I could see it so clearly... *Jesus came to seek and to save everyone who was lost.*

As I eagerly listened to this man preach, I was amazed that of all the years born and raised in a Spirit-filled Charismatic Church I had never heard a message on the simple truth of the gospel. The universal sin of man, the holiness of God and the wrath-bearing sacrifice of Christ may have been believed, but it was never communicated. I guess now that we were all saved saints, the gospel no longer was required. I, however, needed it and remembered drinking in his sermon like water.

When the pastor brought his sermon to a close, he concluded with something to this effect:

> *"In eternity past, long before God spoke the creation of the world into existence, He, in his eternal counsel determined whether to save you or not. In His inscrutable, perfect wisdom God set his love upon you and chose you for salvation. God reached His hand down and plucked "lil ole you," amongst all the depraved sinners in the world, out of the fire. And lest you take credit for it, be certain that the choice of your "chosenness" came directly from God and His sovereign grace. He and He alone made the final decision on your everlasting fate, and nothing can thwart or hinder His saving purposes. If you are saved today is it because God has chosen you by His eternal decree and nothing can snatch you from His hands."*

I did not know it at the time, but this I came to learn was the Gospel of Calvinism. To this preacher it was pure, one hundred percent good news that should leave us humbled and awestruck in wonder at the glorious, saving grace of God. Just think about it. Who would choose such a sinful, depraved, unworthy wretch like me? Surely I wouldn't. But God… (Oh, how those two words made him tingle), who is rich in mercy, predestined each one of us for salvation way before we were even a thought in our parent's mind. Sounds pretty amazing, doesn't it? Who wouldn't worship and bow before a sovereign God such as this?

But as we closed in prayer something happened. Suddenly I began to think of the multitudes all around us who, if this man was right, never had the opportunity for salvation. I thought of the hippy stuck in the 80's standing next to me, and the young, overweight girl in front. I thought of my friends, family, and neighbors who, perhaps in some mysterious, unexplainable way were left unchosen by God and never invited to participate in the salvation-party of the ages.

If the gospel was glad tidings for all people, as he had quoted in Luke 2:10, what about the billions upon billions of people around us whose only choice (which actually wasn't their choice at all) was to be damned by God's eternal decree? This sad bunch never made it to God's list. He knew them from their mother's womb and created them in His image and likeness, but scratched them out of the Book of Life long before they took a living breath. Before they had committed one sin, their reprobate ticket was already punched for the eternal torment of hell.

What about those who have rejected Christ time and time again? Perhaps, if he was right, they were never chosen for salvation in the first place. Maybe God loved them only enough to create them, but not enough to save them. Perhaps they are just where they are, not because they've denied God, but because God had rejected them long before they had the choice to snub Him. Perhaps it would have been better for them to be aborted than taking a living breath.

What about prayer, evangelism, and discipleship? What good is it to weep over the salvation of sinners and labor in proclaiming the gospel to all men, as Scripture commands? If God has already determined who will be saved and made it certain that salvation is *not* for all men, what are we even doing? And who in their right mind would command all men everywhere to repent, as Paul did, if it is utterly impossible for those God has already chosen to harden? Wouldn't such a message be a lie that gives all men a false hope?

I left that gospel service with a lot of unanswered questions, but one thing in my soul was clear. This kind of "gospel" was not for me because it was not good news for all men. It was not until much later that I began to understand that this so-called-gospel did not originate with Jesus Christ, but with a man named John Calvin, from whom we get the theology called Calvinism.

This book is my journey as a student and pastor into the troubled theological waters of Calvinism in light of Scripture and reason. It is both a critique of Calvinism and a defense of Arminianism (the opposite belief, you could say, of Calvinism). Using quotes from leading Calvinist voices, I present their case and use Scripture and counter-arguments to challenge the fallacy of Calvinism's Five Points of theology.

Unchosen is not for theologians and scholars, but for simple students of Scripture who love Jesus and tremble at His Word! I pray this book provokes you to wrestle with the truth of the gospel and that you come to discover the good news of Jesus Christ for all people!

INTRODUCTION

Most Christians are theological Arminians though most do not even know it.[1] They may not call themselves Arminian or even know what exactly that means. In fact, they do not even care about labeling themselves by that title or any for that matter. They are disciples of Jesus, who, after they became saved, read the Bible, believed it, and were never indoctrinated with Calvinist theology.

Jacobus Arminius (the founder of Arminianism) never set out to establish five points of theology. Instead, he and his followers sought to protect the Bible from those who have hijacked the faith with extreme views of sovereignty, free will, and predestination. In the same manner, most believers today only want to defend the plain and straightforward teachings of Scripture. They reject Calvinism *not* because they are "Arminian," but because they love Jesus and honor His Word.

In case you were not aware, there are no self-taught Calvinists! If someone picked up a Bible off the street and read it cover to cover one hundred times, having never been taught it from another, he would be an Arminian through and through. He would believe in the love and sovereignty of God, the sin of man, the invitation for all to be saved, man's ability and responsibility to respond to God in repentance and faith, and the need to persevere in faith until the end. He would not be a Calvinist, Pelagian, or Semi-Pelagian, but a full-blooded Arminian.

Being taught something by another does not imply that it is wrong. However, it does not necessitate that it is right either. To find the truth we must be like the Bereans. Daily we must receive the Word with all readiness and cultivate a lifestyle of diligently searching the Scriptures

---

[1] Being Arminian has nothing to do with the country of Armenia or being Armenian. Arminianism is a theological lens through which we view the doctrines of salvation, historically rooted in the Wesleyan, Holiness movement.

[Acts 17:11]. Testing everything, including our tightly held traditions and beliefs, requires enormous humility. No one wants to admit to being wrong. I know I don't. But the level of our deception, no matter how great or small, can be broken when, and only when, our love for the truth trumps our stubborn pride.

When it comes to theology there are innumerable arguments and counter-arguments, all "based on Scripture." As much as I want to say I am right on every point, I am not. Neither are you. We need to be careful not to major on minors while minoring on the majors. Too many Calvinists, and far too many Arminians, are getting sidetracked from loving Jesus Christ and one another, over endless arguments concerning predestination and free will. Yes, they matter. But at the end of the day, as we stand before Him in judgment, do we really believe He is going to bring up the countless hours that we bashed one another on our Christian blogs in the name of defending the faith?

The world will know we are Christians by our love [John 13:35]. Not by our Calvinism or Arminianism. Not by our pre-tribulationism or post-tribulationism. Not by our Amillennialism or Premillennialism. By our love. There comes a point when we have to love one another and simply agree to disagree. Healthy dialogue is useful and necessary, but there is no place in the kingdom for ugly divisiveness that paints others with whom we disagree as unsaved pagans. We are still brothers and sisters in Christ despite our theological differences.

To be clear, my concern with Calvinism is not with many of the men who believe and teach it. I cannot count the numbers of hours I have spent reading or listening to Sam Storms on the beauty of Jesus, John Piper on the glory of God, Wayne Grudem on a Biblical approach to spiritual gifts, Paul Washer on the gospel, or Mark Dever on Biblical Theology. Though they may not agree with me on every doctrinal point, I admire these men and have learned much from them. I will not call them false teachers or label them as heretics.

Unlike John Calvin's abhorrent and un-Christlike treatment of the apostates of His day, I will not see to their execution and call for them to be burned at the stake.² Like me, these men sincerely love Jesus and seek to honor Scripture. They are fellow brothers who are noble men of the faith, and they are all staunch Calvinists. The very same Scriptures that I see one way, they view through a different lens. As the old illustration goes, when I see a duck, they see a rabbit. So who exactly is the apostate?

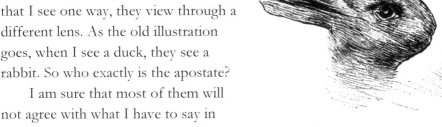

I am sure that most of them will not agree with what I have to say in this book, or appreciate some of the blunt language I use to communicate the logical (or should I say *illogical*) conclusions of Calvinist theology. I get it that most Calvinists won't convert to Arminianism, nor Arminians to Calvinism. However, I also believe that despite our deep differences we can love one another in the grace of God, trusting that He will sort it all out in the end.

THE FUNDAMENTAL DIFFERENCE

Whether we choose to approach Scripture as a Calvinist or Arminian greatly affects our view of salvation, Christ's redemption, and ultimately the nature of God Himself. The theological debate over Calvinism vs. Arminianism is far more significant than who is right and who is wrong. It is about God and His character. The fundamental difference between these two contrasting points of theology is not predestination, election, or free will, but rather the nature of God. Ultimately, it is about who He is and who we believe Him to be.

The debate about Jesus' identity was the same issue facing the disciples of His day [Matthew 16:13-19]. When confronted with all sorts of ideas and rumors as to whom men thought He was, Jesus brought

---

² Calvinism's family secret is that the great John Calvin himself was an unrepentant persecutor and murderer of those whom He considered heretics (See Philip Schaff's *History of the Christian Church - Vol. 8*. Pg. 690,691).

them back to one all-important question: "*Who do you say that I am?*" Jesus wanted to find out what they really believed about Him and what they thought He was like. To Jesus, every other issue was secondary compared to their discovery of His character and nature as God's beloved Son.

As with the disciples, too many people live off of what others say about Jesus. It is not enough that we take our favorite preacher's word for it. We cannot stand before the Lord at the Judgment Seat and say, "Charles Spurgeon said…" or "Paul Washer said…" or "John Piper said…" We must take time to come humbly before the Father in the secret place of prayer, with Scripture in hand, to find out what God says concerning Himself [Matthew 16:17]. Is He love? Is He good? Is He just? Is He perfect? Is He sovereign? Who is this man Jesus of Nazareth who is the perfect image of the Father [John 14:9]?

When all of the theological points, debates, and discussions are over, we face that one soul-searching question, "*Who do you really believe Jesus to be?*" The answer to this is the quintessential reason for this book. Our revelation of God, however accurate or misconstrued it may be, is what Jesus promises to build everything in life and ministry upon [Matthew 16:18]. In other words, our whole foundation of Christianity will be off unless we start with God's nature. Yes, God is powerful, glorious, and sovereign! But He is also good. Very good!

Before we get to the matter of free will and before we pull out our proof texts either for or against Calvinism or Arminianism, we must first get to the matter of Jesus. All arguments are silenced in Him. More important than the doctrines of grace is the doctrine of God. His identity is supreme to every other issue. Do not get side-tracked from this one thing: God's relentless love revealed in the face of Jesus Christ is the foundation of every Evangelical doctrine and theological sub-point.

It also goes to say that the sum of God's attributes never contradicts each other. We do not get to choose between His sovereignty and love, His goodness and wrath, His grace and holiness, His mercy and judgment. It is the whole counsel of God that we must cling to and nothing else. Half-truths or shallow explanations of the *"inscrutable mysteries"* of God cannot do when God has made His character known to

His people, by His Word, and through His Spirit.

False humility says that coming to profound, and convincing theological conclusions about God, His nature, and His plan of redemption are unattainable. Some erroneously say, "Why even concern yourself with such matters? Let's just love Jesus!" They forget that loving Jesus first requires that we know Him as He really is. You cannot love someone you do not know, nor will you love Him rightly if you think Him to be something He is not. Theology always affects intimacy, for better or for worse.

Because of this, all believers are invited to go deep in God and obtain a solid Biblical framework through which we view Him, His Word, and His saving activity in the earth today. Obviously, we will not know everything there is to know about God or how this all works together for our good and His glory. Of course, that is the case when dealing with finite creatures and the Uncreated God. There is much more light that will be revealed to us when we stand before His eyes and see Him face to face. But let me remind you that we can *know* Him.

> 1 John 5:20 "*We know* that the Son of God has come and has given us an understanding, that we *may know Him* who is true… His Son Jesus Christ."

We can *know* the deep things of God.

> 1 Corinthians 2:10 "…*God has revealed* them to us through His Spirit. For the Spirit searches all things, yes, the *deep things* of God."

Christians are not putting God in a religious box when we come up with Biblical and theological convictions by which we stake our life on. God, who Himself cannot be contained, has already put Himself in a box called His Word. Certainly, the Bible does not limit God, nor does it include everything there is to know about Him. He is infinite, eternal and never to be exhausted. However, God has constrained the revelation of

Himself to the sixty-six books of the Bible, giving us everything we need for life, ministry, family, business, discipleship, and worship.[3]

As a pastor of a Spirit-filled Evangelical Church, I am greatly disturbed by our lack of sound Biblical theology when it comes to all important doctrines of salvation. We who have been greatly influenced by the Pentecostal and Charismatic Movement have a reputation for a lot of things (faith, the gifts of the Spirit, lively worship, and unfortunately unusual and unbiblical manifestations), but I am convinced that the central root and source of the problem in our midst is bad theology concerning the gospel.

To our shame, we do not know God because we do not go deep in the Bible. Even worse, we accuse those who do as being "religious." Nevertheless, the Holy Spirit is calling the Church back to the knowledge of God and the supremacy of Scripture. He is inviting us to know once again what we believe, why we believe it, and most importantly Whom it is that we are believing in. Only then will we be fully confident in articulating the glory of Christ's gospel to the ends of the earth.

REFORMED THEOLOGY & NEW CALVINISM

Calvinism is a system of theology that has emerged from the theological beliefs of John Calvin and other Reformation-era theologians. Lutherans who opposed their beliefs and practices first labeled it as Calvinism after their founder, though many Calvinists prefer the more trendy title of being "*Reformed*." Though the Reformed tradition includes man others besides rigid Calvinists, today Calvinism is practically synonymous with Reformed Theology.[4]

---

[3] This doctrine, known as the "Sufficiency of Scripture," tells us that God knows what we can handle as humans at each stage of redemptive history. And though in one sense "God is bigger than His book," we are not to embrace revelations of God that are outside of the Biblical narrative [1 Corinthians 4:6; Revelation 22:18,19].

[4] Not all who call themselves "Reformed" adhere to all of Calvinism's Five Points, but all who call themselves Calvinists lay claim to being those who are 'truly Reformed.'

"Calvinism is a *synonym* for the Reformed tradition."[5]

"Today the terms Reformed and Calvinist are *nearly synonymous*."[6]

At the core of Calvinism is their famous Five Points of theology. The well-known Reformed theologian and Pastor R.C. Sproul wrote the classic book called "What is Reformed Theology?" and systematically lists Calvinism's Five Points and Covenant Theology as being foundational to Reformed faith and doctrine. To him, and many other Calvinist authors, unless you are a TULIP toting Calvinist you are not Reformed in any sense of the word.

The Reformed Calvinist tradition encompasses much more than Calvinism's Five Points. It has hundreds of doctrinal points and convictions. However, at the heart of modern-day Calvinism is an unswerving allegiance to TULIP, an acronym that represents their five theological pillars (see Chapter 1). These pillars shape the way we understand the sovereignty of God, our dilemma of sin, grace and faith, predestination and election, and Christ's atoning work of salvation.

Through the modern-day ministries of Mark Driscoll, Louie Giglio, John Piper, David Platt, Matt Chandler, Kevin DeYoung, and Tim Keller; Calvinism has taken America by storm. Under the title of being "Young, Restless, and Reformed," the gospel according to Calvinism is now hip and relevant again. Even *Time Magazine* has said "Calvinism is back" and listed it as one of the ten ideas that are currently changing our world in the twenty-first century.[7] It is an old dog with a new bark (and bite – if you happen to cross the wrong Calvinist).

This new movement of Calvinism has rightly called the apathetic church back to the supremacy of Scripture, the centrality of the cross, and the glory of God in all things. However, it has also called the church to embrace TULIP radically as if it is the only gospel that truly upholds God's greatness and glory. Millennials have flocked to it by the

---

[5] Kapic & Vander Lugt. *Pocket Dictionary of the Reformed Tradition* (Downers Grove, IL: InterVarsity Press, 2013), p. 29.
[6] Steven Smallman, *What is a Reformed Church?* (Phillipsburg, NJ: P&R Publishing, 2003), p.7.
[7] *Time Magazine*. May 12, 2009.

thousands because they have seen the utter emptiness and spiritual shallowness of the mega-church movement that is light on Scripture, on sin, on regeneration, on holiness, and extremely light on God.

New Calvinism is attractive because it presents a high view of God as an alternative to man-centered Christianity. Our generation of young zealots sees through plastic, seeker-friendly, sinners-prayer religion. In defiance of our empty, counterfeit-church-culture, we have looked for something more authentic, more Biblical, more substantive, and more concrete. However, many are being taught that the only legitimate alternative to our man-centered, mega-church gospel is a God-centered Calvinism.

But is this the only alternative? Is there a God-centered, God-exalting gospel that can contend with the New Calvinism and its radical embracing of TULIP?

There is.

"…There is no such thing as preaching Christ and Him crucified, unless we preach what nowadays is called Calvinism… Calvinism is the gospel, and nothing else." [8]

-C.H. Spurgeon

---

[8] Charles Spurgeon, *The New Park Street Pulpit*, Vol. 1, Sermon: A Defense of Calvinism. 1856.

1

TULIP

Calvinism is the gospel, and nothing else? …Really?

All other views that may confront Calvinism are wrong and not faithful to Christ or Scripture? As much as one loves and admires Spurgeon as the "Prince of Preachers," one has to wonder from where such a proud statement would come. To say that someone is not preaching Christ or Him crucified unless we affirm Calvinism is to say that saints of old like John Wesley, DL Moody, AW Tozer, CS Lewis, and Leonard Ravenhill (who are all Arminians), preached the wrong Jesus and proclaimed another gospel. Ridiculousness!

Arminianism is not a shallow, man-centered gospel. Regardless of what some falsely say, man is not preeminent in the Arminian view of sin and salvation. God is! God's glory, God's sovereignty, God's grace, and God's power are all extolled and exalted above man's self-centered, feeble attempts to bring forth their salvation.

On this point, many Calvinists dig in their heels. For them, Arminianism is Pelagianism at its worst and Semi-Pelagianism at its best. If you have made a stand with Arminianism, you have probably been accused of this somewhere along the line even if you did not initially know what it meant! This mischaracterization is a sad attempt to discredit Arminianism before it is seriously considered. Undoubtedly it would do the Church well to see it compared to its counterparts: Pelagianism (salvation is entirely man's doing) and Calvinism (salvation is entirely God's doing).

THREE SYSTEMS OF SALVATION

Throughout history, there have been three primary theological views or "systems" of salvation. All are very different in what they say about God's role in salvation and man's responsibility.

On one end of the pendulum, we have Calvinism. It says that *God alone saves us*. When He decides to save us, He does so without our help or willing participation. God chooses some to be saved and passes over the rest because He is God and has the right to do so. God gets what God wants and therefore man's salvation- from regeneration to glorification, and everything in between (repentance, faith, and perseverance) is strictly God's doing for God's glory. Man has very little, if any part to play in the process of salvation.

On the other end of the pendulum, we have Pelagianism that says that *we save ourselves*. It is strictly our work, and what we do that earns our salvation. God ultimately has no part in it. Man is somehow inherently good and can "work" or "will" his way closer to God until he is finally saved.

In between these two extremes is Arminianism, which says that both *God and man participate or cooperate in the process of salvation*. Salvation is a work of God and an act of man in responding to God's saving grace. To the Arminian, God is the initiator and author of salvation, yet God does not save man apart from his participation or willing response to God's prevenient grace.

Bible teacher David Pawson made it simple using this helpful, albeit imperfect illustration:

Imagine a tide of raging water going out past the pier. As the people on the pier lookout over the crashing waves, they notice that there are two people in the water being helplessly carried out to sea. They are both dead. Noticing that both bodies are being swept away toward utter destruction, a man on the pier dives in for the rescue. Though he can save both of them, he only chooses one and leaves the other to drown. He drags the body to shore and immediately gives it mouth to mouth until he is brought to life.

This first scenario is a picture of *Calvinism*. The dead man that was bobbing around in the water was rescued by the one who jumped in to save him. The dead man did nothing to "contribute" to his salvation. It was impossible for him to do so simply because he was dead. He could not respond or even want to be rescued. That desire came solely from the one on the pier. Sadly the rescuer (who had the ability to save them both) only chose one, leaving the other to drown in destruction.

Now imagine two other people who were left in the water. Unlike the man who was dead, these two still can respond though they are both on the verge of drowning. Both of them are desperate, helpless and struggling. They cry out, "Save us! Save us! We're going under!" Another man on the pier looks down and says, "No! I will not save you. You can save yourself if you only make a bigger effort! You are good enough! You can do it! Try harder! Keep kicking! Keep swimming! Save Yourself!"

The second scenario is a picture of *Pelagianism*. The rescuer (God) is putting all of the responsibility on the one in the water (the sinner) to save themselves by their self-effort and strength. Though God gives the call, man is essentially the author and finisher of his salvation.

Finally, the other struggling in the water sees another man on the pier throw him a rope with a life preserver. He shouts, "Grab hold, and I will pull you to safety!" The drowning man sees his final chance, grabs the life raft with the last energy that he possesses and is pulled to safety.

The third scenario is a picture of *Arminianism*. It is the balance of the other two, and most importantly it involves cooperation between both God and man. God is the rescuer, but man must take hold of the lifeline. This "synergistic" relationship preserves man's responsibility in salvation and keeps God from being the author of evil. Never will the man who grabs the rope say, "I saved myself by my effort." No! He was rescued by the one who drew him to safety. However, he certainly has a part to play in his salvation, even if it is a very small part.

Without question, Pelagianism is not Calvinism, and neither is it Arminianism. Pelagian's view of salvation and His denial of original sin is heresy. It completely contradicts the plain teaching of Scripture. Our self-efforts or works do not save us. Grace saves us through faith [Titus 3:5;

Galatians 2:16; 2 Timothy 1:9]. One area of agreement between Calvinism and Arminianism is that they both vehemently deny Pelagianism.

Despite the efforts of some Calvinists to accuse Arminians of resurrecting Pelagianism and inserting it into their preaching, they are *not* synonymous. To affirm man's role in responding to God's saving grace and believing in Him for salvation is not legalism or works-salvation [Romans 4:5]. We are not saved by works alone (Pelagianism), nor are we saved by grace alone (Calvinism), but we are saved by grace through faith (Arminianism).

> Ephesians 2:8,9 "By grace you have been *saved through faith*, and that not of yourselves; it is the gift of God, *not of works*, lest anyone should boast."

CALVINISM VS. ARMINIANISM

The division over Calvinism and Arminianism began in the early 1600's between the followers of the French Reformer John Calvin (1509-1564) and the Dutch theologian Jacobus Arminius (1560-1609). Arminius and his followers disagreed with John Calvin's *Augustinian*[9] view of predestination, and in 1610, his disciples presented various counter-arguments to Calvin's doctrines that became known as the *Remonstrance* (i.e., protest).

In 1618 through 1619 the followers of Calvin met at the Synod of Dort to clarify their theological positions in response to the Arminians objections. These Canons of Dort eventually developed into and became known as the Five Points of Calvinism. Today these Five Points are defined by the acronym TULIP:

---

[9] Augustine was the founder of Roman Catholicism and (though born much earlier) was considered the 'spiritual father' of John Calvin. All of Calvin's doctrines were shaped by Augustine's influence.

    T - Total Depravity
    U - Unconditional Election
    L - Limited Atonement
    I - Irresistible Grace
    P - Perseverance of the Saints

Following the Synod of Dort, Arminians were called upon to recant their beliefs and stop confronting Calvinism with their pens and from their pulpits. They refused, and, as a result, Arminian ministers and leaders were prohibited by the state from preaching their anti-Calvinist doctrines and banished from the Church.

The dispute over Calvinism did not stop with the disciples of Calvin and Arminius. Since that time, there has been much division and heated debate between the two camps. Theologian and revivalist John Wesley (an Arminian) and famed preacher George Whitefield (an Arminian turned Calvinist) began in ministry together yet ultimately fell out of fellowship and parted ways over the issue.

> "The Wesley's were unshakable 'Arminians' who denied predestination, yet the revival drew zealous recruits from areas in which Puritan Calvinism was much alive. *At first, Whitefield was no predestinarian*, but by the time he sailed to America in the summer of 1739, he was reading Calvinist books. Contact with fervent American Calvinists filled out his knowledge... John Wesley feared that Calvinism propagated fatalism and discouraged growth in holiness. Charles Wesley feared that predestination (and particularly the idea of reprobation, that God predestined some to damnation) represented a loving God as a God of hate. In his famous hymn *Wrestling Jacob*, he deliberately capitalized the sentence 'Pure Universal Love Thou Art.'" [10]

---

[10] Excerpt is taken from Christianity Today, April 01, 1993, *"Wesley Vs. Whitfield"* by J.D. Walsh, Senior Research fellow at Jesus College, Oxford.

Similarly, Charles Finney, arguably the greatest soul-winner of all time, was raised a Calvinist and eventually rejected it as unbiblical and dangerous to Christian evangelism. Though more Semi-Pelagian in his theology and methodology, than Classical Arminian, Finney was instrumental in bringing forth one of the most profound revivals in Church history as he opposed the error of Hyper-Calvinism. Finney disagreed with Calvinism's extreme views of depravity, slavery of the will, limited atonement and regeneration boldly affirming, "I cannot embrace these views come what will. I cannot believe they are taught in the Bible."[11]

Today Reformed Calvinist leaning ministries and denominations include Reformed Baptists, Particular Baptists, Presbyterians, United Church of Christ, Congregationalists, Evangelical Reformed Church Association, Nine Marks Ministries, Acts 29 Network, Newfrontiers, The Gospel Coalition, and Sovereign Grace Ministries.[12]

Arminian inclined ministries and denominations include Methodists, Church of the Nazarene, Free Will Baptists, Missionary Church USA, The Christian and Missionary Alliance, Brethren in Christ, Mennonites, Wesleyans, Churches of Christ, General Baptists, Calvary Chapel, Vineyard Churches, Assembly of God, The Salvation Army, Pentecostals, and Charismatics.

THE FIVE POINTS OF CALVINISM

The Five Points of Calvinism are a complex system of theology that functions as a whole. There is no such thing as a partial Calvinist or a mixed-breed Calvinian.[13] Leading Calvinist scholars affirm that it is entirely inconsistent to embrace some of Calvinism but not all.[14] Edwin H. Palmer in his well-known defense of TULIP writes, "All the Five

---

[11] Rosell & Dupuis, *The Original Memoirs of Charles G. Finney* (Grand Rapids: Zondervan, 2002), p. 36,37.
[12] The list is not comprehensive, nor does it speak to every individual Church within every denomination. Many Baptists, for example, do not consider themselves Arminian or Calvinist.
[13] A term used by some to advocate a make believe hybrid of Calvinism and Arminianism.
[14] Loraine Boettner, *The Reformed Doctrine of Predestination* (Phillipsburg: Presbyterian and Reformed Publishing Co., 1932), p. 59.

Points of Calvinism hang or fall together."[15]

Though there are some common similarities, Calvinism and Arminianism have very different perspectives through which they view sin, salvation, grace, election, and perseverance. In the following chapters, we will dive deeper into each of Calvinism's Five Points and address some of their inherent problems in relation to the whole of Scripture. However, it will be helpful to look briefly at TULIP compared to its counterpart – Arminianism.

T – TOTAL DEPRAVITY

Calvinism teaches that we are radically depraved and because of our sin we *cannot* do anything to *respond* to the Gospel. Total Depravity is often referred to as "Total Inability," implying that our depravity is so great that we cannot and will not choose God with our free will unless God first makes us willing through regeneration. We are free to do a lot of things, but we are not free to turn to Christ in repentance and faith. Calvinism says that to be saved God must first cause us to be born again before we make any willing choice to repent and believe.

Arminianism teaches that we are radically depraved and need God's prevenient grace to be saved. Nevertheless, unregenerate men still have a God-given conscience that, assisted by grace, gives them the *ability* and the *obligation* to respond to God as an act of our will. Our depravity is severe and total, yet it does not take away our responsibility in salvation. Sinful men are dead in sin and spiritually separated from God, yet grace frees our will to choose or reject God's offer of salvation.

U – UNCONDITIONAL ELECTION

Calvinism teaches that *God decides who gets saved and who does not regardless of the person*. Before you were born and had the ability to choose Him God decided your eternal salvation or damnation. Therefore, election is without condition. There is nothing you can do to obtain

---

[15] Edwin H. Palmer, *The Five Points of Calvinism* (Grand Rapids: Baker Book House, 1980), p.69.

salvation for it was already determined by the eternal decree and counsel of God. God in His sovereign grace chooses to rescue some sinners while leaving the rest of humanity to perish eternally.

Arminianism teaches that *God decides who gets saved based upon the person's response of faith to His call.* Unlike Calvinism, God does not arbitrarily choose to save some and damn most because He foreordained it, but because some responded to His call and most did not. Arminians firmly believe that mankind's election is conditional based upon the foreknowledge of God (i.e., God knows who will repent and believe). Election speaks of God's choosing of a people in Christ (the Church) made up of individuals who freely and willingly repent of their sins and put faith in Jesus. Therefore, election is both a corporate promise and an individual call.

L – LIMITED ATONEMENT

Calvinism teaches that *Christ did not die for everyone*, but only for the elect. The cross does not make the salvation of all men possible; instead, it uniquely and exclusively saves the elect. Calvinists believe that the atonement is *sufficient* for all, but it is *limited* to those whom God had already chosen for salvation. This view is also called "Particular Redemption." God has a particular, limited number people whom He has chosen to redeem (the elect) thereby making the saving work of the cross only effectual on their behalf.

Arminianism teaches that *Christ died so that all men might be saved*. He died for all, desires all men to be saved, has no pleasure in the death of the wicked and therefore commands all men everywhere to repent and believe the gospel. What Jesus accomplished through His death and resurrection is not limited and effectual for only a few, but is offered to all men everywhere. Arminians believe that the atoning work of Christ is both *sufficient* and *available* to all who respond in repentance and faith, though they affirm that not all people will be saved.

I – IRRESISTIBLE GRACE

Calvinism teaches that grace is not an undeserved favor, but an *irresistible force*. If God sovereignly and unconditionally elects whom He desires to save, He, therefore, makes sure their salvation by irresistibly drawing them to Christ. In other words, God brings the elect to Himself simply because He has chosen them, not because of their willing participation or cooperation. Calvinists assert that the sinner maintains their freedom in salvation, yet God's saving grace sovereignly changes our wills so that we gladly and freely respond. The new birth is entirely God's work wrought upon a sinful heart through the power of the Holy Spirit, before our repentance and faith.

Arminianism teaches that grace is not an irresistible force, but an *underserved favor*. The saving grace of God enables us to respond to His supernatural drawing which produces in us a heart of repentance. Man does not save himself but is saved by grace through faith as a gift of God. Arminians affirm that saving grace is both powerful and prevenient, but it is never forced upon us by God. God does not bypass the human will, nor does the Holy Spirit force our will to be willing. Instead, He draws us to Himself in love and through His grace works together with man's conscience in bringing forth our eternal salvation. God ordained that His grace could be resisted by our choice.

P – PERSEVERANCE OF THE SAINTS

Calvinism teaches that those who are *elect are preserved by God* and therefore will *persevere in holiness to the end*. Those who are truly saved are eternally secure. Nothing and no one, including yourself, can separate you from His loving hands. If you are one of the few that is sovereignly elect, and if He has irresistibly drawn you by His grace, it follows that you will necessarily persist in faith firm to the end. Nothing can hinder you from being saved simply because you've been chosen from the foundations of the earth. Unconditional Election logically results in unconditional Perseverance. If perhaps someone who seems to be a believer does "fall away" into sin or unbelief, it proves that they were never actually elect in the first place.

Arminianism teaches that once you start the Christian faith God enables and supernaturally gives the grace to persevere until the end *if you continue to believe*. A true believer has nothing to worry about as long as they remain in the faith of Jesus. The power of God keeps the people of God *through faith* unto salvation. However, the Arminian view of perseverance is not divine, unconditional preservation, but the active participation of the believer through continual trust in Jesus and obedience to His commands. God calls, sustains, and rewards believers for keeping His command to persevere and He also continually warns genuine believers of the danger of falling away and suffering shipwreck concerning the faith. Therefore, our assurance is real but conditional. It is possible for a true Christian to fall away from God and commit apostasy fully and finally, only one time, and thereby lose their salvation.

CONTEND FOR THE FAITH

There are many other views concerning salvation than rigid Calvinism and Arminianism as just described. Some Calvinists only believe in four points of TULIP, except Limited Atonement. Some Arminians hold fast to unconditional eternal security. I want to be careful not to lump everyone into one group or the other, but rather highlight their primary views in contrast to one another. Though one may not agree with every narrow point of each system, most believers stand on either side of this debate, affirming most beliefs but not necessarily all.

Without a doubt, Jesus will bring more light on this controversy when He comes the second time to reign with His saints on the earth. God will have the final word! Until then, we must humbly, passionately, and prayerfully address the core issues; daring to ask difficult questions concerning the Biblical testimony of the glorious gift of salvation. God is inviting us to be a people who contend earnestly for the faith and labor for His heart regarding the common and at times complex doctrines of salvation.

Jude 1:3 "Beloved, while I was very diligent to write to you concerning our *common salvation*, I found it necessary to write to you exhorting you to *contend earnestly for the faith* which was once for all delivered to the saints."

"One of the reasons that God makes human babies small is so that they won't kill their parents in their sleep. They're evil!"

- Voddie Baucham

2

DEPRAVITY

Humanity is radically depraved! That debate is over. It was forever finished with the canon of Scripture. Even if one never read the Bible, they could pick up a local newspaper and determine that the root of our problem is a three letter word called S-I-N. We may deny it, but we cannot escape it. Sin is a universal human condition.

But how radical is our depravity? That is a big question because it shapes our Christianity and the gospel that we preach. Is it true that God made babies small so they won't slit their parent's throat while they are fast asleep, as Calvinist Pastor Voddie Baucham described in a sermon on *The Doctrine of Total Depravity*? Is this the view of sin found in Scripture?

To answer this question, we will be helped by going back to the Word and starting from the beginning. The Bible says that in our lost, sinful state we know nothing but sin. Our thoughts, attitudes, actions, and our very nature are corrupt to its core. No matter how "good" we may think we are, one look at God's Law shows us that there is only One who is good, God alone [Matthew 19:17]. Our whole being is under the power and influence of sin.

> 2 Chronicles 6:36 "For there is *no one* who does not sin…"
>
> Romans 3:23 "*All have sinned* and fall short of the glory of God,"
>
> Psalm 143:2 "In Your sight *no one* living is righteous."

> Romans 3:10-12 "As it is written: 'There is *none righteous*, no, not one; There is none who understands; There is none who seeks after God. They have all turned aside… There is *none who does good*, no, not one.'"

Joel Osteen, Oprah Winfrey, Mahatma Gandhi and Mother Teresa are considered as some of the most exceptional people to have ever lived, yet in God's eyes, they (apart from Him) are sinners of the worst sort. Like all of us, they are born in sin and wicked from their youth. Nothing good dwells in them apart from the grace of Jesus.

Because of the fall, all men are born morally corrupt [Genesis 3]. Sin binds us and enslaves us to evil passions. Sin is all around, and when we look within we see it filling the very core of our being. It is a dark, and deadly plague that left untreated will produce all manner of death and destruction- spiritually, emotionally, relationally and physically. The passing pleasure of sin always brings forth lasting damage to all who indulge it [James 1:13-15].

Sin is not just something that we do; it is who we are deep in our heart [Matthew 15:18]. We are born in sin and bound to its condemnation. Ask any parent, and you will quickly discover that you do not have to teach a little child to be unruly. By nature, it is what they are. We have to instruct them to be good and do good, and after all that, we find they still need more discipline.

> Psalm 51:5 "Behold, I was brought forth in iniquity, and *in sin my mother conceived me*."

> Psalm 58:3 "The wicked are estranged *from the womb*; they go astray as soon as they are born, speaking lies."

> Romans 5:12 "Just as through one man sin entered the world, and death through sin, and thus death spread to all men, because *all sinned*."

> Genesis 8:21 "The imagination of man's heart is *evil from his youth...*"

As a result of our sinful condition, we are separated from God and unable to please Him. We have no hope and are without God in the world [Ephesians 2:12]. Having broken His Law- the Ten Commandments- we are by our very nature children of wrath [Ephesians 2:3; James 2:10]. As long as our sin remains in the court of heaven, we will stay at odds with God, and our rebellion will testify against us all the way to hell. What fellowship does light (God's holiness) have with darkness (man's depravity)?

Arminius himself did not shy back from the severe reality of our depravity when he said,

> "In his... *sinful state*, man is not capable, of and by himself, either to think, to will, or to do that which is really good; but *it is necessary for him to be regenerated and renewed* in his intellect, affections or will, and in all his powers, by God in Christ through the Holy Spirit, that he may be qualified rightly to understand, esteem, consider, will, and perform whatever is truly good."[16]

Without the saving work of Christ even our very best works, done apart from Him, are but a stench in His nostrils. All of our acts of righteousness are like filthy rags [Isaiah 64:6]. Though they put on an outward show of piety, beneath the facade is one who is corrupt to his core. A leper remains a leper no matter how much he may spend on his wardrobe.

THE HEART OF THE GOSPEL

Any serious follower of Jesus understands the sin and depravity of man is

---

[16] Jacobus Arminius, *Complete Works of Arminius*, Volume 1, Public Disputations of Arminius, Declaration of the Sentiments, 5:3

at the heart of the gospel! If we are by nature good, and if evangelism is "pulling out the good in people" (as I have recently heard taught by a famous Charismatic evangelist) what need is the cross? And what is the point of repentance, confession of sin, or sanctification? Why should we confront our sin and turn from it with zeal if God doesn't see our sin, but only sees our human goodness and potential?

Jesus said that He doesn't call the righteous, but sinners, to repentance [Matthew 9:13]. A sinner will not repent if they do not first see and come to terms with the fact that they are, as far as God is concerned, a criminal who has offended God and broken His Law. When someone doesn't know they have cancer, it does them no good to tell them you found their cure. They will think you're nuts. However, if you took the time to show them their symptoms and prove how deadly their cancer is, they would rejoice at the cure and treasure the good news with their life.

Sadly, this is where Pelagius got off track with works salvation. His affirmation of man's inner goodness and denial of original sin distorted his entire vision of grace, salvation, and redemption. In his eyes, man could draw near to God on his own, apart from grace, which the Bible declares is utterly impossible! To lessen sin, and take it out of the equation will single-handedly dismantle the gospel that Jesus and the Apostles taught in Scripture. Both Evangelicals and Charismatics are guilty of this treachery. We have cut man's depravity out of our message altogether, for the sake of gaining popularity and church growth.

Here we find the central problem with much of the mega-church movement. We are afraid to talk about sin and have unwittingly taught a false form of salvation (called sinners-prayer-Pelagianism) that teaches men to accept Jesus and pursue their best life now, while ignoring their cancer called sin. However, any gospel that does not address the sin of man is not the gospel!

> 1 Corinthians 15:3 "Christ died *for our sins* according to the Scriptures,"

Galatians 1:4 "Who [Christ] gave Himself *for our sins*…"
1 Timothy 1:15 "Christ Jesus came into the world *to save sinners*, of whom I am chief."

On this point, I highly value the contribution Calvinism has brought to the body of Christ. Calvinists, by all means, are not weak on sin. They see depravity not as a side issue, but the core issue. I have yet to meet a Calvinist, who has not held the ground on man's utter sinfulness and need for salvation through Jesus Christ. However, many Calvinists have taken the depravity of man to an extreme, which has brought unbiblical and misleading conclusions about the nature, purpose, and means of salvation that God desires to bring to all people.

REDEFINING TOTAL DEPRAVITY

All true believers believe in the depravity and sin of man! The problem is not with the doctrine of depravity but what exactly we mean when we say it. Arminians and Calvinists view man's depravity much differently though both call it *Total Depravity*. Some have said they affirm the "T" in TULIP because of their conviction in the utter sinfulness of man. I believed this for a season until I understood the full theological implications of Calvinism's Total Depravity.

Calvinists define Total Depravity as sinful humanity being so depraved that we cannot save ourselves. The word "total" can be misleading because it does not claim that all humans are as evil as they could be but that our entire being is profoundly affected by sin. All non-Calvinists affirm this and could not agree more.

However, Calvinism's definition of Total Depravity is not primarily the understanding of man's sinful condition, but rather his "Total Inability" to believe the gospel that they speak of. Calvinists view man's sinfulness as more than the fact that we are utterly corrupt, but that *our sinfulness takes away our ability to respond to God's grace in repentance and faith*.

Rather than focusing on man's sinfulness and need for the gospel, Calvinists use Total Depravity to promote Calvinism. By concentrating on man's inability to believe freely in Jesus for salvation, they seek to galvanize the other points of TULIP, namely Unconditional Election and Irresistible Grace. Rarely if ever will you hear of a Calvinist simply focus on man's depravity and sin. Instead, they try to highlight and stress the supposed outcome of man's depravity – Total Inability.

According to Calvinism, the depravity of man is not describing the sinful condition of man and the immoral acts that he does but instead is used to describe that man is unable to repent and believe unless first born again. Depravity is not so much an affirmation of man's sin, but the denial of his free will. By deliberately concentrating on man's inability, Calvinists now have the proper framework to promote their version of predestination.

Certainly, Calvinists do not deny free will in its fullness. They admit that unbelievers everywhere still choose every day to do evil and maintain their freedom to practice wicked deeds, yet that very freedom given to them by God is taken away from them when it comes to salvation. As a Calvinist friend once said, "In our depravity, we are free to do a lot of things- including evil, but we are not free to choose God in any form or fashion." Calvinist teacher and radio host Dr. James White declared,

> "[In Paul's conversion] God's grace paid *no heed to Paul's "free will"*; it overwhelmed him, changed him, resurrected him, and gave him a new heart- *without Paul's assistance.*"[17]

Spurgeon also affirms Calvinism's definition of Total Depravity and free will saying,

> "*Free will is nonsense…* I will go as far as Martin Luther, where he says, 'If any man ascribes anything of salvation, even the very least thing, to *the free will of man*, he knows nothing of grace, and he has not learned Jesus Christ rightly."[18]

---

[17] James White, *Debating Calvinism* (Colorado Springs: Multnomah Books, 2004), p. 205.
[18] Charles H. Spurgeon, *Free Will – A Slave* (Canton: Free Grace Publications, 1977), p. 3.

Calvinism's love affair with Total Inability is out to undermine man's responsibility in salvation thus proving Calvinism's error of Unconditional Election. Here again is the single most important reason they care about defending depravity. The fact that we are sinful is not an issue, but what matters is that we cannot and will not respond to the gospel ever, unless we are first sovereignly and irresistibly born again by God.

To prove Calvinism's argument, they often point to various prooftexts that demonstrate the fact that sinful man cannot choose God and turn to Him with repentance and faith but only do according to his nature, which is to choose to remain in his sin.

> Matthew 7:17,18 "Even so, every good tree bears good fruit, but *a bad tree bears bad fruit.* A good tree cannot bear bad fruit, nor can a bad tree bear good fruit."

> Matthew 12:35 "A good man out of the good treasure of his heart brings forth good things, and *an evil man out of the evil treasure brings forth evil things.*"

Anyone would agree with Jesus that a rotten tree bears bad fruit, and the heart of an evil man brings forth evil things. But does a rotten tree (an unbeliever) *only* bear bad fruit (sin)? And does a healthy tree (a believer) *only* bear good fruit (live a sinless life)? No! All Calvinists would emphatically disagree with the idea that believers, once saved, are given the *ability* to live a sin free life; yet they are free to apply the same logic to unbelievers when it comes to salvation. However, in the context of Matthew 7, Jesus was not talking about all unbelievers for all time, but false prophets who looked one way and acted another.

The same logic pertains to Jesus' reference in Matthew 12. Does an evil man (an unbeliever) *only* bear evil things (sin), and does a good man (a believer) *only* bear good things (live a sinless life)? No! We know this is not the case simply because Paul himself affirmed that as a believer, his will was still under the influence of sin that dwells in him. Like all of us, though he willed to do good, many times he did the very opposite [Galatians 5:16,17]. Paul's supposed inability that was irresistibly overcome at his salvation was still present and at war within him after regeneration.

> Romans 7:15-21 "For what *I will to do*, that I do not practice; but what I hate, that I do. If, then, I do what *I will* not to do, I agree with the law that it is good. But now, it is no longer I who do it, but sin that dwells in me. For I know that in me (that is, in my flesh) nothing good dwells; for *to will is present with me*, but how to perform what is good I do not find. For the good that *I will to do*, I do not do; but the evil *I will not to do*, that I practice. Now if I do what *I will not to* do, it is no longer I who do it, but sin that dwells in me. I find then a law, that evil is present with me, the one who *wills to do* good."

To prove that sinful man has no willful choice in his salvation, the Calvinist goes on the offensive in attacking Arminianism. They assert that the Arminian, who believes in a freed will, denies the work of the Holy Spirit in regeneration and promotes works-salvation. However, no faithful Arminian would ever affirm that the sinner who is desperately wicked can change his own depraved heart by his willpower and strength.

It is God alone who changes our hearts, and He does so without coercion. All who receive Him by trusting in His name, He gave the right to become the sons of God [John 1:12,13]. God's will always works together with man's willingness before one is supernaturally born of Him. The free will of man in salvation implies that sinners, through the conviction of the Holy Spirit and prevenient grace of God, have the *ability* to repent and receive Christ; whereby God always responds in giving us the new birth.

SIN AND DIVINE GRACE

The Arminian view of Total Depravity is much different than Calvinism's extreme emphasis on man's Total Inability. Arminians insist that we are radically depraved, dead in sin, and doomed to destruction. Therefore, God must take the initiative in salvation. To be saved we need God's prevenient, drawing, enabling grace. Without it, our cold hearts will not respond to His fire or turn to Him in sincere repentance.

Despite our utter sinfulness, unbelievers still have a God-given conscience that can be pricked and convicted by the Holy Spirit. The fall does not render the conscience of a man obsolete. Every person to some level has an inner "check" in his heart that initially lets him know, in some measure, the difference between right and wrong, good and evil. It testifies to the fact that man is responsible to a moral law that is set forth by God Himself.

> John 8:9 "Those [unbelieving scribes and Pharisees] who heard it, being *convicted by their conscience*, went out one by one."

The fact that unbelievers still retain a conscience is found all throughout Scripture. Though is it is defiled [Titus 1:15], sinful [Hebrews 10:22], and seared [1 Timothy 4:2]; nevertheless it remains, which is why fallen men do not sin in the fullest possible sense every day. They have a God-given conscience written on their hearts that acts as a restraining influence and leaves them without excuse before God, even if they have never heard the gospel.

> Romans 1:20 "For since the creation of the world His invisible attributes are clearly seen, being understood by the things that are made, even His eternal power and Godhead, so that they are *without excuse*."

> Romans 2:14,15 "When Gentiles, who do not have the law, by nature do the things in the law, these, although not having the law, are a law to themselves, who *show the work of the law written in their hearts*, their *conscience also bearing witness*, and between themselves their thoughts accusing or else excusing them."

Because the Holy Spirit is continually at work, and sinful men still have a conscience, all men, therefore, have the *ability* and the *obligation* to respond to God's saving grace. Affirming such a truth does not lessen our depravity or heighten our belief in works-salvation. However, it does fly in the face of Calvinism's Five Points and disarms every other argument to which Calvinists cling.

Lest we are found guilty of following Calvinism's mistake of focusing on the *result* of our depravity, it will be helpful to step back and look at how the Arminian views man's Total Depravity.

> "Humanity… fell from its original sinless state through willful disobedience, *leaving humanity in the state of total depravity*, sinful, separated from God, and under the sentence of divine condemnation… Sin impacts every part of a person's being and that people now have a sinful nature with a natural inclination toward sin. Human beings are… corrupt at heart, …spiritually dead in sins, …and slaves to sin. Thus, human beings are not able to think, will, nor do anything good in and of themselves. *We are unable to do anything that merits favor from God, and we cannot do anything to save ourselves* from the judgment and condemnation of God that we deserve for our sin. We cannot even believe the gospel on our own. *If anyone is to be saved, God must take the initiative.*"[19]

Calvinists have often accused non-Calvinists of being light on the sin of man. However, one glance at the words of faithful Arminians throughout history will prove that this is anything but the case. Consider the bold stance of Jacob Arminius concerning man's radical depravity and the absolute necessity of Divine grace in salvation.

> "In this state [of depravity], the free will of man towards the true good is not only wounded, maimed, infirm, bent, and weakened;

---

[19] Brian Abasciano. *The FACTS of Salvation: A Summary of Arminian Theology.* www.evangelicalarminians.org.

but it is also imprisoned, destroyed, and lost. And *its powers are not only debilitated and useless unless they be assisted by grace, but it has no powers whatever except such as are excited by Divine grace*. For Christ has said, 'Without me ye can do nothing.'"[20]

In our depravity the free will of man is wounded, imprisoned, and lost. No man can will or work his way into the Kingdom alone. We must be assisted and enabled by God's grace. Here the saving, convicting work of the Holy Spirit bears upon our conscience and draws us to repentance. Nevertheless, unlike Calvinism, we are not sovereignly forced into the relationship. We are invited to the wedding and drawn with cords of lovingkindness, but not coerced against our will.

> Matthew 22:3 "[The Master] sent out his servants to call those who were invited to the wedding; and they were *not willing* to come."

Whether we like it or not, human willingness (our voluntary choice to respond to God's drawing grace), is often associated with salvation in Scripture. On many occasions, Jesus rebuked unbelievers for their unwillingness to come to Him and submit to God's will.

> John 5:40 "But *you are not willing to come to Me* that you may have life."

> Matthew 23:37 "…How often I wanted to gather your children together, as a hen gathers her chicks under her wings, but *you were not willing*!"

> Luke 7:30 "The Pharisees and lawyers *rejected the will of God* for themselves…"

---

[20] Jacobus Arminius, *Complete Works of Arminius*, Volume 1, Public Disputations of Arminius, Disputation 11 (On the Free Will of Man and its Powers).

Revelation 22:17 "*Whosoever will*, let him take the water of life freely."

Freedom of the will is essential because God has established relationship on the basis of voluntary love from the beginning of time. God can do a lot of things, but He is not in the robot manufacturing business. From Genesis to Revelation we see a God, who wants friends that chose to love Him because they want to, not because they have to, as a result of Irresistible Grace.

A perfect example of this is found in the case of Lydia's conversion [Acts 16:14,15]. Lydia did not save herself or work up her salvation through womanly grit. God opened her heart to heed the gospel spoken by Paul. Nowhere in this text do we find God forcing Lydia to be saved because she was sovereignly elect, nor do we find any trace of God regenerating her heart before she repented and believed. We must be content with what Scripture says without adding into it our theology: The Lord opened her heart to heed the things spoken by Paul, and she and her house were saved.

ARE SINNERS UNABLE TO TURN TO CHRIST?

Calvinists defend humanity's Total Inability to respond to God's grace in repentance because we were "dead in sin" as unbelievers [Galatians 4:8,9; Titus 3:3; Romans 6:6, 17-18; 7:14; 2 Timothy 2:25,26]. And as they say, "dead men are utterly incapable of willing anything," let alone trust in Christ for salvation.[21] However, being dead physically, as in the case of Lazarus, cannot be compared to someone who is *actually alive* (possessing a living conscience and will) though they are spiritually dead.

The New Testament passages about humanity being dead in transgressions and sin is a figure of speech that speaks to our spiritual separation from God [John 8:34; Ephesians 2:1,2; Colossians 2:13]. Being dead in sin as unbelievers is the opposite of being alive in Christ as believers. Jesus used this analogy when describing the parable of the lost

---

[21] A. W. Pink. *The Sovereignty of God*, (Edinburgh: The Banner of Truth Trust, 1961), p. 141.

son. His son was *dead* in sin though still physically alive, now having returned to his father's house, he is *alive again*. Jesus was simply stating the fact that the prodigal was separated from his Father and out of His life-giving relationship.

> Luke 15:24 "For this *my son was dead and is alive again*; he was lost and is found."

In like manner, Jesus rebuked the Church in Sardis saying, *"You have a name that you are alive, but you are dead! Wake up!"* Though He calls them "dead" they were still living, breathing humans. Their apparent deadness spoke of their separation from God, not their lack of free will. They could again choose life, spiritually speaking, by watching and strengthening the things that remained.

> Revelation 3:1 "I know your works, that you have a name that you are alive, but *you are dead*. Be watchful, and strengthen the things which remain…"

Despite the typical Calvinist claim, no text of Scripture speaks of being dead in sin as referring to our inability to make real choices to follow Christ or deny Him [2 Timothy 2:12]. Instead, we are encouraged time and again to choose life. God commands this because a living man though spiritually dead still has a will that can be awakened with supernatural grace.

> Deuteronomy 30:19 "I have set before you life and death, blessing and cursing; therefore *choose life*."

> Joshua 24:15 "*Choose for yourselves* this day whom you will serve."

If man in his sin is utterly unable to respond to Christ without the Holy Spirit manipulating our heart and forcing us to obey, why are there so many Scriptures that urge sinful men to turn from their sin unto

Christ? Notice how each of these passages highlight man turning to God with his will, rather than God turning man to Him against his will.

> Isaiah 55:7 "*Let the wicked forsake his way*, and the unrighteous man his thoughts; let him return to the LORD, and He will have mercy on him; and to our God, for He will abundantly pardon."

> Ezekiel 18:23 "Do I have any pleasure at all that the wicked should die?" says the Lord GOD, "and not that *he should turn from his ways* and live?"

> Ezekiel 33:11 "Say to them: 'As I live,' says the Lord GOD, 'I have no pleasure in the death of the wicked, but that the wicked turn from his way and live. *Turn, turn from your evil ways*! For why should you die, O house of Israel?'"

Think for a minute of your conversion. Were you automatically born again and given spiritual life before you repented and believed? Or did you sense the Holy Spirit's powerful, drawing, prevenient grace and respond to Him with deep repentance and faith that perhaps He might save you and make you new?

From Genesis through Revelation we find multitudes of passages that speak of God's call to the unregenerate man to "come unto Him." An invitation such as this would make no sense if depravity meant that it was something we cannot actually do with His assistance. God would not command *all men* to turn, repent, call upon Him, and seek Him if it were only possible by a select few (the elect) who were sovereignly enabled by His Irresistible Grace.

> Psalm 50:15 "*Call upon Me* in the day of trouble; I will deliver you, and you shall glorify Me."

> Psalm 86:5 "For You, Lord, are good, and ready to forgive, and abundant in mercy *to all those who call upon You*."

Matthew 11:28 *"Come to Me, all* you who labor and are heavy laden, and I will give you rest."

John 7:37 *"If anyone thirsts,* let him come to Me and drink."

Luke 13:23,24 "'Lord, are there few who are saved?' …And He said to them, *'Strive to enter* through the narrow gate…'"

Acts 17:26 "[God] has determined their preappointed times and the boundaries of their dwellings, so that they should *seek the Lord, in the hope that they might grope for Him and find Him,* though He is not far from each one of us."

One has to wonder why God would continually call sinful men to repentance if they were morally or spiritually unable to do so. Why would Jesus call every man to "strive to enter" through the narrow gate of salvation if it were essentially impossible for the totally depraved? Why would Paul seek to persuade men with the gospel if they could not ultimately be persuaded [2 Corinthians 5:11]? And why would he plead with men to be reconciled to God if God already determined not to reconcile them [2 Corinthians 5:20]?

Why should we plead, persuade, or preach at all? According to Calvinism, it is utterly pointless unless God has already chosen beforehand to draw the elect and save them alone. If men could be persuaded, they would then be contributing to their salvation, and their salvation would rest upon their response of faith, not Christ's sovereign grace. Why not just sit around and wait for God to save us since we are unable to do anything – including believe?

RESPONDING TO GRACE BY FAITH

The Bible from beginning to end tells us that man, in his radical depravity, when, and only when, he is drawn by God, has the *ability* and the *obligation* to respond to God's saving power by which he repents and believes. The will of the Father is that *everyone* who sees the Son and believes in Him, may have everlasting life; yet *no one* can come to Jesus unless the Father first draws him.

> John 6:40,44 "This is the will of Him who sent Me, that *everyone* who sees the Son and *believes in Him* may have everlasting life... *No one can come* to Me unless the Father who sent Me *draws him*; and I will raise him up at the last day."

Our response of faith is not something that we conjure up on our own. Believing in Jesus and receiving the gift of salvation requires no effort or ability on our part. However, it does require God's supernatural drawing and the surrendering of our will to the supremacy and lordship of Christ.

The followers of Arminius accurately said,

> "Man does not have saving faith of himself, nor out of the powers of his free will, since in the state of sin he is able of himself and by himself neither to think, will, or do any good (which would indeed to be saving good, the most prominent of which is saving faith)... We hold, however, that *the grace of God is not only the beginning but also the progression and the completion of every good*, so much so that even the regenerate himself is unable to think, will, or do the good, or to resist any temptations to evil, apart from that preceding or prevenient, awakening, following and cooperating grace. *Hence all good works and actions which anyone by cogitation is able to comprehend are to be ascribed to the grace of God...* The will in the fallen state, before calling, does not have the power and the freedom to will any saving good."[22]

Oh, the glory of prevenient grace! God's saving grace goes before us to draw every man to Himself, unlock our sinful hearts, and convict us of

---

[22] *The Opinions of the Remonstrants* (1618) regarding the third and fourth articles, concerning the grace of God and the conversion of man, sections 1, 2, and 4.

our need for a Savior! In the end, we who are saved will have nothing to boast about but Jesus Christ and Him crucified.

> John 12:32 "And I, if I am lifted up from the earth, will *draw all peoples to Myself.*"

*"We do not believe in order to be born again;
we are born again that we may believe."* [23]

-R.C. Sproul

---

[23] R.C. Sproul, *Chosen by God* [Wheaten: Tyndale House. 1986], p. 73

3

REGENERATION

Every Super Bowl Sunday I find it fascinating, and quite entertaining, to hear believers root for football teams they would otherwise despise because they have more born again Christians than the other. It's as though God favors the players with eleven real, Spirit-filled Christians over the team with ten. Apparently, the losers lost because they didn't have enough heavenly mojo in their huddle that made them run faster, throw better, and tackle harder.

As ridiculous as this example seems it underscores how cliché the term "born again" has become. It has lost its true Biblical power in our generation. People everywhere slap on its title and can name our favorite born again sports hero, but few have experienced its life-changing power. To be clear, the term "born again" was not coined by Russell Wilson or Kevin Durant. It came from the lips of Jesus Christ in John 3 when he said (and I summarize), "Unless one is born again, he cannot perceive or enter the kingdom of God."

> John 3:3-6 "Jesus answered and said to him, 'Most assuredly, I say to you, *unless one is born again, he cannot see the kingdom of God.*'" Nicodemus said to Him, 'How can a man be born when he is old? Can he enter a second time into his mother's womb and be born?'" Jesus answered, 'Most assuredly, I say to you, unless one is born of water and the Spirit, *he cannot enter the kingdom of God. That which is born of the flesh is flesh, and that which is born of the Spirit is spirit. Do not marvel that I said to you, You must be*

born again.'"

Being born again is essential to our understanding of the gospel. When we are regenerated, our heart is spiritually changed and transformed from its wicked, godless state and made new by the power of the Holy Spirit. Scripture calls this interior experience the new birth, being born again, born of God, regenerated, born of the Spirit, or made alive in Christ [1 Peter 1:3].

When salvation begins in each one of us, God takes away our heart of stone and gives us a new heart that is soft and tender towards Him. Our filthiness is washed, and our conscience is cleansed. A new spirit is given to us - the fullness of God's Spirit dwelling within us. Through the new birth, we are instantly changed (though not perfected) because of God's indwelling presence and power.

> Ezekiel 36:25-27 "I will cleanse you from all your filthiness and from all your idols. I will give you a *new heart* and put a *new spirit* within you; I will take the heart of stone out of your flesh and give you a heart of flesh. I will put My Spirit within you…"

Biblical regeneration is nothing less than a complete transformation of the entire person from the inside out. It is no small thing. God Himself has come to dwell with us and in us. We are now His full possession, coheirs with Christ, seated in heavenly places, adopted into His family, recipients of His spirit and partakers of His divine nature.

Sadly, much of the Church today has replaced true spiritual regeneration of the heart with a magical sinners-prayer that one has mindlessly to repeat in order to be saved. This quick and easy method of conversion may work to persuade unbelievers into the Church, but it will not give them a new heart, nor bring them into the Kingdom. They *must* be born again! As Jim Cymbala, senior pastor of the Brooklyn Tabernacle rightly concludes,

> "Churches meeting right now, today, are *filled with people who are not born again*, but their meetings are such that they will never be pricked to the heart, they will never be disturbed; they are going in and out of church every Sunday, and *they will end up making their bed in hell.*"[24]

Because we have not taught Biblical regeneration, we have millions of people attending Churches week after week, year after year, who have never experienced the inward life, joy, and power of God in their daily lives. They are Christian in name, but not in deed and action. They are religious, but not spiritual. They have a form of godliness, but deny its saving power [2 Timothy 3:1-5]. True Calvinists and Classical Arminians agree that it is high time that we return to what the Bible says will genuinely save a man: The regenerating power of the Holy Spirit.

REGENERATION BEFORE CONVERSION?

For many years, having read the Bible through over and again, though never taught Calvinism nor Arminianism, I believed that for a man to be saved, he must first respond to God's drawing grace by repenting of His sins and believing on the Lord Jesus. These verses and many others like them were clear on this fundamental truth:

> Acts 16:30,31 "'Sirs, what must I do to be saved?' So they said, '*Believe on the Lord Jesus Christ, and you will be saved*, you and your household.'"

> Mark 16:16 "He who *believes* and is baptized *will be saved.*"

> Luke 8:12 "The devil comes and takes away the word out of their hearts, lest they should *believe and be saved.*"

> 1 Corinthians 1:21 "It pleased God… to *save those who believe.*"

---
[24] Jim Cymbala. Sermon: "*The Caller,*" preached October 10, 2004, tape #PO1492N.

> John 20:31 "These are written that you may believe that Jesus is the Christ, the Son of God, and *that believing you may have life* in His name."

> Romans 10:9 "If you confess with your mouth the Lord Jesus and *believe* in your heart that God has raised Him from the dead, you will be *saved*."

Believe and be saved! …How confusing can it be? Scripture after Scripture made plain that genuine repentance and faith preceded being born of God's Spirit. Though God loved me while I was yet a sinner, there was no impartation of saving, divine life until I repented and believed in the gospel. There was no forgiveness without repentance, no regeneration without faith. It was evident to me that believing in the Lord Jesus and trusting in Him for salvation is the way that one becomes His child and is supernaturally born of Him.

> John 1:11,12 "He came to His own, and His own did not receive Him. But *as many as received Him,* to them He gave the right to become children of God, *to those who believe* in His name."

John, the Beloved Apostle, taught and believed as I did. In the Gospel of John, he affirmed that anyone who receives Christ and *believes* in His name becomes His child and is born into the family. By believing in the light, one *becomes* a son of light. The verb *"become"* is crucial because it demonstrates the obvious progression of salvation. Believing always precedes becoming a son who has eternal life through His name.

> John 12:36 "While you have the light, *believe in the light*, that you *may become* sons of light."

> John 20:31 "These are written that you may believe that Jesus is the Christ, the Son of God, and *that believing you may have life* in His name."

Similarly, the Apostle Paul proclaimed that the gospel is the power of God unto salvation to them that believe. Through the means of hearing, receiving, and believing the gospel message, one is begotten of God and born again. Real saving faith, marked by true repentance, is the medium by which we become recipients of genuine regeneration.

> Romans 1:16 "For I am not ashamed of the *gospel* of Christ, for it is the power of God to salvation for *everyone who believes*, for the Jew first and also for the Greek."

> 1 Corinthians 4:15 "For in Christ Jesus I have *begotten* you through the *gospel*."

I was convinced that true repentance and faith preceded salvation not only because it was made plain to me in Scripture, but because my testimony affirmed it. While I was deep in sin, I sensed God's drawing power and knew that something was not right. I was aware deep down that I had offended Him. His righteous law was bearing down heavily on me. If I was to be in proper relationship with God, I must repent of my sin and believe in Jesus. By doing this, I found spiritual life and began to walk on the narrow way many years ago.

My conversion reminded me of the multitudes crying out to Peter, "What shall *we do* to be saved?" Having been cut to the heart and convicted by the Spirit, Peter called all of them to repent and be baptized for the forgiveness of sins so they could receive everlasting life. Notice that they could *do something* if they were to be saved. In response to God's drawing grace, each of them not only had the ability to do so, but they were commanded to *do* it if they were to receive the forgiveness of sins.

> Acts 2:37-40 NIV "They were cut to the heart, and said to Peter and the rest of the apostles, "Brothers, *what shall we do?*" Peter replied, "*Repent* and be baptized, every one of you, in the name of Jesus Christ for the forgiveness of sins. And you will receive the gift of the Holy Spirit… And with many other words he warned

them; and he pleaded with them, '*Save yourselves* from this corrupt generation.'"

It was not until years later, having come across a Hyper-Calvinist that I understood how off I was in my beliefs. When asked the question, "What can man do to be saved?" he boldly and unashamedly claimed, "There is absolutely nothing you can do... God does it all!" Having nearly fallen off my seat from being slain in the spirit (by a spirit that wasn't the Holy Spirit), I finally realized the difference between a Calvinist and Hyper-Calvinist. Though they both believe the same theological framework, the Hyper-Calvinist puts into practice what he believes.

But was I off in thinking that one must believe in order to be saved? If so, why didn't Peter say, along with the Hyper-Calvinist, "There's nothing you can do to be saved... God does it all!" Instead, Peter called all of them to repent and be baptized for the forgiveness of sins so that they could receive the Holy Spirit. Even worse Simon Peter proceeds to add a blasphemy upon blasphemy, according to the Hyper-Calvinist, in saying, "*save yourselves* from this crooked generation" [Acts 2:40].

Save Yourselves? There is no statement more hated by Calvinists than that! The Calvinist, if they were true to TULIP, would say that there is nothing *you can do* to become saved. God alone saves man and that without our help.[25] Did you hear that? There is *nothing* you can do- unless you happen to be one of the elect! You cannot repent and believe until you are first regenerated by God and born of His Spirit! God must do it all from beginning to end if He is to get all of the glory!

Consider the words of John Calvin, R.C. Sproul, and John Piper,

> "Faith does not proceed from ourselves, but is the fruit of spiritual regeneration; ...*No man can believe, unless he be begotten of God.*"[26]

---

[25] Calvinists call this "monergism," the idea that God alone brings about salvation without the involvement of man.
[26] John Calvin, Calvin's Commentaries (Grand Rapids: Baker Books, 2009), p. 43-44.

> "Unless we first receive the grace of regeneration, we will not and cannot respond to the gospel... *Regeneration must occur first* before there can be any positive response of faith." [27]

> *"We do not think that faith precedes and causes new birth.* Faith is evidence that God has begotten us anew." [28]

While denying Hyper-Calvinism in practice, the rigid Calvinist fully embraces its belief. To prove Total Depravity and Unconditional Election, the instantaneous act of spiritual regeneration (the imparting of saving divine life) must precede repentance and faith. As they say, one will not and indeed cannot believe or exercise any faith in Christ unless he first be born again. This order of salvation is necessary for TULIP to work and preserves the Calvinist belief that God alone chooses man, man does not choose God.

To validate their claims, Calvinists like John MacArthur, again point to proof-texts to show that God does the choosing and not man.[29] After all, did not Jesus say, "*You did not choose Me, but I chose you* and appointed you that you should go and bear fruit and that your fruit should remain, that whatever you ask the Father in My name He may give you" [John 15:16]?

Why is it that all of the intellectually challenged non-Calvinists never get this verse? It is not difficult. Jesus said, "You did not choose Me, but *I chose* you." Jesus alone does the choosing in salvation! But does not John's Gospel say earlier that Jesus "chose" the twelve and one of them is a devil? How does this fit with Calvinism's view of predestination and regeneration? Was Judas also "chosen" for salvation by a secret, sovereign decree of God?

---

[27] R.C. Sproul, *What is Reformed Theology?* (Grand Rapids: Baker Books, 1997), p. 186.
[28] John Piper, *TULIP: What We Believe about the Five Points of Calvinism* (Minneapolis, Minn.: Desiring God Ministries, 1997), www.desiringgod.org.
[29] John MacArthur, *What is the Doctrine of Election?* (Grace to You Ministries, Article, 2015), www.gty.org.

> John 6:70 "Jesus answered them, 'Did I not *choose you*, the twelve, and one of you is a devil?'"

We must be careful not to read into our favorite texts more than they say. In its proper context, Jesus' phrase *"You did not choose Me, but I chose you"* has nothing to do with God's electing purposes for salvation. Rather Jesus chose the twelve and appointed them to be apostles, including Judas, who would go and bear fruit for His name [Mark 3:14]. Only in this context could Jesus say that He "chose" Judas, though knew he was a devil and doomed to destruction.

OBSESSION WITH ORDO SALUTIS

Calvinism's single greatest proof-text concerning God choosing man for salvation through a sovereign work of regeneration is found in 1 John 5:1. John Piper in his TULIP DVD teaching series uses this verse it to verify Calvinism's order of salvation by saying, "Whoever has been born of God… believes!" Like many other Calvinists who change the *ordo salutis*[30] in Scripture, he fails to recognize that John's point in writing 1st John is not to prove the order of salvation but to show what someone who is indeed born of God looks like [2:29; 3:9; 4:7; 5:1]. Whoever believes will be born of God and whoever is born of God will believe. This verse can be taken either way and is hardly conclusive evidence of salvation irresistibly happening before one puts faith in Jesus.

> 1 John 5:1 *"Whoever believes* that Jesus is the Christ is *born of God."*

Any serious student of theology will soon recognize that Calvinists obsess over the order of salvation in order to defend TULIP and prove Calvinism. But why does it matter so much that we show to believers who are already saved that regeneration precedes faith unless we are zealous to convince them of Calvinism? Does it help us in evangelism

---
[30] Latin for the "order of salvation."

and proclaiming repentance and faith to the lost [Acts 20:21; Hebrews 6:1]? Does it help us in preaching that calls all men to repent and believe the gospel, just as Jesus did with the multitudes, if they will be saved regardless by a sovereign decree of regeneration [Mark 1:15]?

Calvinists have a hard time proving their ordo salutis in Scripture. There are simply no clear examples in the New Testament that the born-again experience takes place before we repent and believe. It is not in the Gospels. Not in Acts. Not in the Epistles. In fact, multitudes of Scriptures say the exact opposite [Acts 16:31; Romans 1:6, 10:9; Luke 8:12; John 3:15, 5:24, 6:40, 6:47; 11:15; 20:31; Hebrews 10:39].

But this begs the question… If we are born again before repentance and faith, why are they even necessary? If they are right, we already have His imparted life. We are already born of God's Spirit. We are already born of God and birthed into His family. We were already saved according to Titus 3:5, the moment we were regenerated and renewed by the Holy Spirit!

> Titus 3:5 "Not by works of righteousness which we have done, but according to His mercy *He saved us, through the washing of regeneration* and renewing of the Holy Spirit'"

Charles Spurgeon, himself a Calvinist, admitted that *"A man who is regenerated… is saved."*[31] Being born again is not separate from salvation. It is salvation itself at its beginning stages, bringing us into a new life – the life of the Spirit- through the means of repentance and faith. In spite of that, Calvinism confounds the confusion once again by saying that regeneration is a magical change wrought in the elect based on a heavenly lottery (a change that he is not even aware of) that produces repentance and faith in the heart, by which a man is saved.

Jesus' teaching on the necessity of being born again in John 3 never mentions the idea that regeneration precedes our believing but that we simply must be born again by God if we are to enter the Kingdom. How

---

[31] Spurgeon, *"The Warrant of Faith," New Park Street Pulpit* (Pasadena, Tex.: Pilgrim Publications, 1978), p. 3.

does this happen? Jesus Himself tells us: By believing in Him.

> John 3:7,15,16 "You must be born again. ...*Whoever believes* in Him should not perish but have eternal life... For *whoever believes* in Him should not perish but have everlasting life."

Ask yourself... If we are regenerated and already saved, according to the words of Paul and Spurgeon, before repentance and faith, why repent? And why believe? Scripture commands us to do so because they are necessary before spiritual regeneration takes place in the heart of sinful man.

> 1 Corinthians 1:21 "It pleased God... to *save those who believe*."

Calvinists do not believe that God saves "them that believe," rather God saves those whom He has sovereignly elected. As they often claim, "People are not born again because they believe, they believe because they are born again." It bears repeating that Calvinism teaches that a man cannot and will not believe – ever; unless God first regenerates his heart and makes him born again.

As stated in the previous chapter, Calvinism's argument for Total Depravity says that our sin removes one hundred percent of our ability to respond to God unless we are first regenerated by God apart from our participation. A sinful, depraved person, even with the help of God's power and grace, cannot put one ounce of faith in Jesus unless they are regenerated and brought to life by the indwelling power of the Holy Spirit. It is impossible! Therefore, they must not only be born again against their wills, but given repentance, and given faith as sovereign, irresistible gifts.

To Calvinists, the Arminian position of man's *ability* and *obligation* to respond to God's prevenient grace through repentance and faith somehow implies that we are contributing to our salvation and mixing it with works. However, it does not take works to believe, simply because faith is not works. God does not justify (or declare a person righteous) by any work that he does, but by believing. Justification is the fruit of faith, not a sovereign product of regeneration.

> Romans 4:5 "To him who does *not work but believes* on Him who justifies the ungodly, his *faith is accounted for righteousness*."

Receiving the gift of salvation by faith takes no work. A gift is a gift. It requires no effort to obtain a present from another and unwrap it. All the work was done in purchasing it for the recipient, but to open it and receive its blessings takes no effort. Nor would the one who is receiving the gift say, "I purchased this for myself." In the same manner, salvation is a free gift offered to all men, purchased for us by Christ and given to us without effort through faith in Him.

> Romans 5:18 "Through one Man's righteous act *the free gift came to all men*, resulting in justification of life."

> Romans 6:23 "The wages of sin is death, but *the gift of God* is eternal life in Christ Jesus our Lord."

HOW DID OLD TESTAMENT SAINTS BELIEVE?

Spiritual regeneration is a New Covenant reality first spoken of by the lips of Jesus and made manifest by the coming of the Holy Spirit at Pentecost. Old Testament saints believed God and experienced a measure of the Holy Spirit's grace and power, but they were not born again [1 Peter 1:3,10; Hebrews 11:39,40].

No Scripture tells us that Old Testament believers were regenerated by the Holy Spirit in the same manner as believers after the cross. Neither does Scripture tell us that our depravity is worse than theirs. And yet all of them exercised faith without regeneration! Hebrews 11 is the famous "Hall of Fame of Faith" that speaks of men and women, who believed and trusted entirely in God for their salvation, yet were never born again.

Hebrews 11:4 "By *faith* Abel…"

Hebrews 11:5 "By *faith* Enoch…"

Hebrews 11:7 "By *faith* Noah…"

Hebrews 11:8 "By *faith* Abraham…"

Hebrews 11:11 "By *faith* Sarah…"

Hebrews 11:20 "By *faith* Isaac…"

It is ironic that all Old Testament saints were commended for their faith (without the new birth) and given the promise of salvation for it, yet now according to Calvinism, it is impossible for one to exercise even an ounce of faith unless one experiences regeneration first. On the contrary, we see that believers in the Old Testament were called, expected, and able to live a life of faith without the Irresistible Grace of sovereign regeneration.

Genesis 15:6 "*He believed in the LORD*, and He accounted it to him for righteousness."

Exodus 14:31 "Israel… feared the LORD, and *believed the LORD* and His servant Moses."

Psalm 13:5 "I have *trusted* in Your mercy; My heart shall rejoice in Your *salvation*."

Jonah 3:5 "The people of Nineveh *believed God*…"

Habakkuk 2:4 "The just shall live *by his faith*."

We also find that Old Testament believers, though radically depraved, were also called to "seek" after Him apart from the new birth experience. God created all men and sovereignly determined their times and dwellings so that they might "seek the Lord, in the hope that they might grope for Him and find Him" [Acts 17:26,27]. These verses and multitudes of others like them would make absolutely no sense if Calvinism's extreme position on Total Inability and regeneration were true.

Amos 5:4 "Thus says the LORD... '*Seek Me* and live.'"

2 Chronicles 15:2 "The LORD is with you while you are with Him. If you *seek Him*, He will be found by you; but if you forsake Him, He will forsake you."

Jeremiah 29:13 "You will *seek Me* and find Me, when you search for Me with all your heart."

Even worse, Calvinism says that not only does God cause unresponsive unbelievers to be born again without their involvement but that repentance and faith are also entirely God's doing. Apparently, this preserves God's glory when we realize that we cannot do a thing- not even repent and believe. Salvation is entirely Him from beginning to end.

To defend TULIP's view of Total Depravity, Calvinists must also teach that repentance and faith are themselves irresistible gifts of God. As Calvinist pastor Sam Storms says, "The Bible portrays faith and repentance as God's gifts to his elect."[32] In other words, if one repents and believes it is because God made him do so based on his election from the foundation of the earth. If one does not repent and believe, He is doing what God has never given him the ability to do. God has chosen to withhold it from him because of His "secret will."[33]

---

[32] Sam Storms, *Chosen for Life* (Grand Rapids: Baker Book House, 1987), p. 46.
[33] Calvinists maintain that God's secret will is His "hidden" and sovereign decree to save only the elect, whereas His revealed will is His "open" desire to save all men [2 Peter 3:9]. It says that God decrees what He doesn't desire so that He is most glorified.

But does the Bible clearly and infallibly prove that repentance and faith are bestowed upon some and not others based upon God's electing grace? Again Calvinists point to a few (and there are only a few) proof-texts to validate their position.

> Acts 5:31 "Him God has exalted to His right hand to be Prince and Savior, *to give repentance to Israel* and forgiveness of sins."
>
> Acts 11:18 "God has also *granted to the Gentiles repentance* to life."
>
> 2 Timothy 2:25 "In humility correcting those who are in opposition, if God perhaps will *grant them repentance*, so that they may know the truth."
>
> Ephesians 2:8,9 "For by grace you have been saved through faith, and that not of yourselves; it is *the gift of God*, not of works, lest anyone should boast."
>
> Philippians 1:29 "For to you it has *been granted* on behalf of Christ, not only to *believe in Him*, but also to suffer for His sake."

The first three supposed Calvinistic passages are often quoted to show repentance being a gift of God and the last two to faith. But on closer examination, we see that none of them bolsters Calvinism's claim of sovereign regeneration based on Irresistible Grace.

If God *giving repentance* to a sinner is synonymous for Calvinism's coerced regeneration, one must necessarily conclude that *all* Jews and *all* Gentiles will be saved, since God has granted it to them [Acts 5:31; 11:18]. One must also concede that Paul's statement in Second Timothy makes no logical sense. If Paul were Calvinist, God would not *perhaps* grant someone repentance that they might know the truth, but would do so with a power that is irresistible and unhindered.

As for the irresistible faith passages, any serious student of Scripture knows that the "gift of God" often spoken of by Paul does not refer to a gift of faith itself. The gift is eternal life offered freely to all men [Romans 5:15-18; 6:23; Acts 2:38, 10:45; 11:17; Ephesians 2:8; Hebrews 6:4]. God, granting men to believe in Him on behalf of Christ and suffer for His sake, never implies that God forces depraved sinners to believe and neither does it guarantee that every believer is also forced to experience extreme suffering, as in the case of the Philippians, for Christ's sake.

God grants repentance to the sinner by drawing and convicting him through His Spirit. Repentance is never something that we do on our own, but by His Spirit and with the help of God's prevenient grace. The Arminian does not believe that sinful man grits his teeth and somehow works up repentance unto salvation on His own. Neither will he make up verses (which there aren't any) to say that regeneration precedes repentance and faith.

Yes, God calls and draws! But man responds. There is not one verse in Scripture that says that man in his unregenerate state cannot and will not respond to the gospel and believe in Christ with the help of His grace. God alone regenerates and gives life to man, when and only when man repents and believes the gospel!

"The chief difficulty with the doctrine of Election, of course, arises in regard to the unsaved."

-Loraine Boettner

4

ELECTION

Election is a glorious truth found all throughout Scripture!

It is deep, profound and mysterious. More importantly, it is thoroughly Biblical! Election is not a Calvinist belief or an Arminian belief. It is a Christian belief. God, not John Calvin, or any other theologian for that matter, has defined the nature and purpose of the believer's election. Therefore, God requires that we *know* and understand it [Matthew 24:22, 24, 31; Mark 13:20, 22, 27; Luke 18:7; Romans 8:33, 9:11; 11:7, 15; Colossians 3:12; 2 Timothy 2:10; 1 Peter 1:2; 2:6; 5:13; 2 Peter 1:10].

> 1 Thessalonians 1:4 "*Knowing*, beloved brethren, *your election* by God."

In its simplest form, election refers to the process and the people whom God has chosen to receive the benefits of salvation. Election answers the question of who God has chosen, why He has chosen them and the means by which they, and not others, will receive eternal life. In the same way that we decide and elect who will serve our country in political office, so God chooses who will be saved based upon His just and loving judgment.

The Christian doctrine of election says that God's people (those who believe the gospel and are saved) are His special people. They are His! God has selected and chosen them for His eternal purpose and glory, and are, therefore, set apart by His grace. The corresponding truth is that those who do not believe, and are not saved, are not elect. They are not God's children and neither will they receive the covenant blessings of eternal life.

> Luke 18:7 "Shall God not avenge *His own elect* who cry out day and night to Him?"
>
> Romans 8:33 "Who shall bring a charge against *God's elect?*"
>
> Mark 13:27 "Then He will send His angels, and gather together *His elect…*"
>
> Titus 1:1 "Paul, a bondservant of God and an apostle of Jesus Christ, according to the faith of *God's elect* and the acknowledgment of the truth which accords with godliness."
>
> 1 Peter 2:9 "You are a *chosen* generation, a royal priesthood, a holy nation, *His own special people*, that you may proclaim the praises of Him who called you out of darkness into His marvelous light."

Arminians and Calvinists agree on this point. Both sides drink in the doctrine of election with delight, yet not surprisingly they both see it through a very different lens. As straightforward as Biblical election seems so much theological nonsense has bogged down the ordinary believers understanding of this great truth. Calvinists have made election out to be larger than Jesus and claim it as their own, rather than a valuable revelation that belongs to every faithful believer in Christ. It has now become a hidden and obscure secret that cannot be understood except by intellectually trained, enlightened Calvinists.

Regardless of what men say, the subject of election is not complicated. It is clear and straightforward to understand. The Holy Spirit is very skilled at helping the ordinary believer grasp its glorious truth. I assure you there is no secret revelation here. God is not the author of confusion [1 Corinthians 14:33; James 3:16]. Election simply reveals that God determines who will be saved, and He has given us in Scripture the means by which He does so.

The great debate concerning the nature of Biblical election is not whether God has chosen people to be saved, but the means (the why and the how) through which He has chosen them. Calvinists say that God decides who gets saved and who doesn't regardless of the person. Election is all God's sovereign choice. From eternity past, God chose to create a few people for heaven (the way is narrow) and created most for hell, all to the praise of His glory!

If you cannot grasp that truth, as many Christians cannot, just deal with it! Who are you, O man, to question God? Who are you to resist His will? It is not easy to look at your little children and think that quite possibly God has decided only one for salvation and the remaining three for eternal destruction just because He is God and has the power to do so. And yet this is what the Calvinist boldly proclaims when he teaches his version of election. God is most glorified in flexing His muscles and damning most to hell, rather than offering the free gift of salvation to all men equally without prejudice.

But is this the Biblical truth concerning the great doctrine of election? First, let me state that most Christians utterly reject this view. They refuse it not because they do not believe that God is sovereign, but because it makes God look more like the Devil than the loving, sovereign Savior who shed His blood on Calvary's tree. No one has described this better than John Wesley's rant in his famous sermon called "Free Grace."

> "One might say to our adversary, the devil, 'You fool, why do you roar about any longer? Your lying in wait for souls is as needless and useless as our preaching is. Do you not hear that *God has taken your work out of your hands*, and that He does it much more effectually?'
>
> 'You, with all your principalities and powers, can only so assault that we may resist you, but He can irresistibly destroy both body and soul in hell! You can only entice; but His unchangeable

decrees, to leave thousands of souls in death, compels them to continue in sin until they drop into everlasting burnings.'

'You tempt; He forces us to be damned, for we cannot resist His will. You fool, why go about any longer seeking whom you may devour? Do you not hear that *God is the devouring lion*, the destroyer of souls, the murderer of men?'

'Moloch caused only children to pass through the fire, and that fire was soon quenched; or, the corruptible body being consumed, its torment was at an end.' But *God, you are told, by His eternal decree fixed before they had done any good or evil, causes not only children… but the parents also to pass through the fire of hell, 'the fire which shall never be quenched.'* And the body which is cast into it, being now incorruptible and immortal, will be ever consuming and never consumed, but, because it is God's good pleasure, 'the smoke of their torment ascends up forever and ever.'"[34]

At the end of the day we are left with one question: *Is this the revelation of God found in Scripture?* I want to be careful but extremely honest here. Some have made the error of saying that Calvinists serve a different God as if it were another cult or false religion. Not so! Calvinists serve Jesus Christ and seek to honor His Word. However, their system of theology and all-out embracing of TULIP demand that they present the God of the Bible in a way that damages His very nature, degrades His love, and distorts His justice.

WHY DOES GOD SEND SINFUL MEN TO HELL?

Calvinism calls this point *Unconditional Election*. It is the "U" in TULIP and one of their most critical beliefs concerning salvation. It is the heart and soul of their theology. Calvinists find it comforting to know that

---

[34] John Wesley. *The Essential Works of John Wesley* (Uhrichsville, Oh: Barbour Publishing, 2011), p. 695.

God has chosen them not based upon anything they have done but only because of God's sovereign grace. They are His special people, sovereignly chosen and selected by Him without condition.

As noble as it seems, non-Calvinists are repulsed by this view because it has a nasty flip side. It implies that if God has unconditionally elected some to be saved, God has also created and predestined the rest to suffer an eternity in hell based on His sovereign choice. This belief is called *Reprobation*. Some Calvinists deny this is the case, yet to believe one it is inevitable to believe the other. If God is sovereign over all, as they say, the very people who are "passed over" and not selected for salvation, are chosen to be damned.

John Calvin himself affirmed,

> "Many indeed (thinking to excuse God) own election, and yet *deny reprobation*; but this is quite silly and childish. For *without reprobation, election itself cannot stand*; whom God passes by, those he reprobates. It is one and the same thing."[35]

> "We say, then, that Scripture clearly proves this much, that God by his eternal and immutable counsel *determined* once for all those whom it was his pleasure one day to admit to salvation, and those whom, on the other hand, *it was his pleasure to doom to destruction*. We maintain that this counsel, as regards the elect, is founded on his free mercy, without respect to human worth, while those whom he dooms to destruction are excluded from access to life by just and blameless but at the same time, incomprehensible, judgment."[36]

To put it rather bluntly, Calvinism maintains that God decided to create billions of people, knowing that they had no possibility of salvation in the first place (because they were not elect), and send them to burn in hell forever all for His glory and good pleasure!

---

[35] John Calvin, *Institutes of the Christian Religion*, 3:23:1 (Peabody, Mass: Hendrickson Publishers, 2008), p. 625.
[36] Ibid. 3:21:7. p. 613.

God did not merely permit men to go to hell forever and ever for their sin. Instead, He *wanted* them to. Therefore, He ordained their damnation and made it happen by His eternal decree. They had no other option because God gave them no other. If He wanted them saved, He would have chosen them to go to heaven, or at least made it available to them. But they are reprobate! He never selected them and for that reason, and that reason alone, they will burn in hell for an endless eternity.

This dreadful quote by John Piper has to top the list of things you do not say at a Baby Dedication!

> "*Before you were born* or had done anything good or bad, *God chose* whether to save you or not."[37]

However, for Piper, this is a crucial point. It answers the question of *why* God sends people to hell. Calvinism asserts that sinful men do not go to hell for rejecting the gospel or on account of their depravity, but because they are merely not elect [Revelation 14:11,12; 2 Thessalonians 1:8,9]. From before time, long before the reprobate were even born or committed one willful sin, they were doomed to destruction and destined for the eternal fires of hell. This destiny was set, determined, and fixed for them by God Himself. God created them uniquely for this, and somehow He is glorified in their everlasting burnings!

It makes one wonder how the Calvinist can argue that the lost deserve God's wrath for living in rebellion to Him if they truly believe that they were sovereignly chosen to be un-elect long before sin entered the world.[38] If their unrepentant sin and hardness of heart is the sole basis of their eternal judgment, would that not make their election to damnation conditional? As F. LaGard Smith writes, "If the 'saved elect' do not deserve their salvation because it is unconditional, how can it be said that the 'lost elect' deserve their destruction?"[39]

---

[37] John Piper, *Five Reasons to Embrace Unconditional Election*. July 9th, 2013. www.desiringgod.org/blog.
[38] F. LaGard Smith, *Troubling Questions for Calvinists*. (USA: Cotswold Publishing, 2007), p. 182.
[39] Ibid.

It does not take much to see why non-Calvinists abhor this view of God. God, viewed through this lens, begins to sound and act more like Hitler than the God and Father of the Bible. However, God looks far worse than Hitler, for the fires of Auschwitz were only for a short moment of time compared to the eternal torment of the wicked. Again I ask, is this the nature God revealed in the Person of His Son?

Arminianism confronts this evil portrait of God and teaches election much differently. Yes! God does decide who gets saved, but His decision is based upon the person's response of faith to His call. Arminians call this *Conditional Election*. There are clear and defined Biblical conditions to being God's elect, namely a willing heart that responds to the Holy Spirit's conviction by repenting and believing in the gospel [Mark 1:14,15; John 5:40; Revelation 22:17].

DOUBLE PREDESTINATION

The Calvinist view of Unconditional Election is also a theological term called *Double Predestination*. As stated earlier, it implies that if God has predestined from eternity some for heaven, He also predestined some for hell for His glory and good pleasure. God chose who would be saved and whom He would pass over (leaving them unsaved) because He is God and has the power and right to do so.

The Westminster Confession declares,

> "The rest of mankind, *God was pleased*, according to the inscrutable counsel of His will, whereby He extendeth or *withholdeth mercy* as He *pleaseth*, for the glory of His sovereign power over His creatures, to pass by, and *to ordain them to dishonor* and wrath for their sin, to the praise of His glorious justice."

Was God *pleased* to pass by and withhold salvation from certain sinners for His glory? Was He pleased? Ancient creeds and confessions may say so, but not Scripture!

Ezekiel 18:23 "'*Do I have any pleasure* at all that the wicked should die?' says the Lord GOD, 'and not that he should turn from his ways and live?'"

Ezekiel 18:30-32 "'Repent, and turn from all your transgressions, so that iniquity will not be your ruin. Cast away from you all the transgressions which you have committed… For *I have no pleasure* in the death of one who dies,' says the Lord GOD. 'Therefore turn and live!'"

2 Peter 3:9 "The Lord is… *not willing that any should perish* but that all should come to repentance."

1 Timothy 2:3,4 "God our Savior… *desires all men to be saved* and to come to the knowledge of the truth."

    There is no denying that predestination is a Biblical term. But it is often misunderstood as God's eternal decree of who goes to heaven and who goes to hell regardless of the person. Understood this way a Pastor can only hope that the members of his congregation for whom he had prayed, labored, and pleaded with for years upon years, were chosen for salvation in the first place. If God took pleasure in not choosing them from eternity past, all of his labors no matter how noble were pointless and in vain [Galatians 4:11].

    Calvinism's view of predestination may be comforting for a Calvinist, who is assured of his special election, but it is not reassuring for the rest of us who just might be doomed from the womb. And sadly there is nothing we can do about it. Calvinism says that God had fixed and set your salvation or damnation apart from you, long before you were born. Yes! It would have been better for you who were reprobate to be aborted than to have been conceived as one of the un-elect only to store up wrath for the day of wrath and revelation of the righteous judgment of God [Romans 1:18-20; 2:5-11].

    Parents, consider this… What if God chose one of your children for salvation and passed by the others for His good pleasure? Would you find delight in God sending your precious offspring to hell while saving another just because He predestined it from the foundation of the earth? No! You would not find pleasure in it, and neither does God!

To take it further, if Unconditional Election were true, what good is it to train our children, equip them, or even call them to salvation if they will be saved or condemned based on the sovereign, unconditional, Irresistible Grace of God? What is the point of praying and travailing for their souls, if God has essentially already fixed their fate whether we do anything or not?

Why should we call all men to repent and believe the gospel if the good news was never meant to be for all men? Why would Jesus say, "Come to Me, *all* who are weary and heavy-laden, and I will give you rest," if He already knew and ordained that *all* could not come in the first place unless they were elect [Matthew 11:28]? This portrait of Christ makes him look like a deranged deceiver! He calls and invites all, though He secretly knows that God has previously slammed the door on most of them having foreordained them to everlasting destruction.

On the contrary, Jesus said,

> John 10:9 "I am the door. If *anyone* enters by Me, he will be saved…"
>
> Matthew 16:24 "If *anyone* desires to come after Me, let him deny himself, and take up his cross, and follow Me."
>
> John 7:37 "If *anyone* thirsts, let him come to Me and drink."

I could never understand why some Calvinists insist on being functional Arminians yet take pride in being theological Calvinists. If one truly believes in a theology of double predestination, by all means, live, function and minister in light of this horrid truth. But for Pete's sake do not use an Arminian methodology and call all men to be saved, and then proceed to teach the new believers in the discipleship class how they "really got saved" - through Calvinism's Unconditional Election and Irresistible Grace.

> "Call it therefore by whatever name you please, election, preterition, predestination, or reprobation, it comes in the end to the same thing. The sense of all is plainly this, — *by virtue of an eternal, unchangeable, irresistible decree of God, one part of mankind are infallibly saved, and the rest infallibly damned*; it being impossible that any of the former should be damned, or that any of the latter should be saved.
>
> But if this be so, then all preaching is futile. It is needless to them that are elected; for they, whether with preaching or without, will infallibly be saved. Therefore, the end of preaching… is void with regard to them; and it is useless to them that are not elected, for they cannot possibly be saved: They, whether with preaching or without, will infallibly be damned. The end of preaching is therefore void with regard to them likewise; so that in either case our preaching is vain, as you hearing is also vain.
>
> This then, is a plain proof that *the doctrine of predestination is not a doctrine of God*, because it makes void the ordinance of God; and God is not divided against himself."[40]

THE BIBLICAL VIEW OF ELECTION

Unconditional Election is not the Biblical view of predestination. Simply put, predestination means that God has decided beforehand to elect *people* in Christ. It refers to the entire Body of Christ made up of individuals who put faith in Him for salvation. Never in Scripture does it refer to God's eternal decree of all men for all time who go to hell or

---

[40] John Wesley, *The Essential Works of John Wesley* (Uhrichsville, Oh: Barbour Publishing, 2011) p. 687, 688.

heaven based upon His sovereign choosing. Read the words of Paul carefully,

> Ephesians 1:4-6 "*He chose us in Him* before the foundation of the world, that we should be holy and without blame before Him in love, *having predestined us* to adoption as sons by Jesus Christ to Himself, according to the good pleasure of His will, to the praise of the glory of His grace…"

Under the inspiration of the Holy Spirit Paul says that He chose us, God's people, *in Him* before the foundation of the world. He predestined us to adoption as sons by Christ Jesus to Himself. In other words, the good pleasure of His will is that all who join themselves to Christ through faith are now eternally *His* and hidden *in Him*. It is only because we are *in Him* by faith that we are His elect people and sealed with the Spirit of promise. As long as we are in Christ, the Elect One, are we elect [Isaiah 42:1].

> Ephesians 1:11-12 "*In Him* also we have obtained an inheritance, being *predestined according to the purpose of Him* who works all things according to the counsel of His will, that we who first trusted in Christ should be to the praise of His glory. *In Him* you also trusted, after you heard the word of truth, the gospel of your salvation; in whom also, *having believed, you were sealed with the Holy Spirit of promise.*"

Election was never meant to be a grand mystery of who God had graciously chosen for salvation and who God has chosen to pass over and condemn to hell. Let me repeat… We were never to ponder the question… "Is this person predestined to salvation? Or are they predestined to hell?" Nor were we ever to assume someone was beyond salvation and predestined to damnation because they have rejected the gospel time and time again.

The true doctrine of election leads us to conclude that if we are *in Christ* through faith, we are elect, chosen, and predestined for salvation according to the eternal purpose and foreknowledge of God. This is not difficult to understand. Scripture repeatedly affirms that Biblical election or predestination is based upon God's omniscient foreknowledge. But who exactly does He foreknow? None other than those who believe and are saved [1 Peter 1:2-9]!

> Romans 8:29 "Whom He *foreknew*, He also *predestined*…"

> John 6:64 "'But there are some of you who do not believe.' For *Jesus knew from the beginning* who they were who did not *believe*, and who would betray Him."

> 1 Peter 1:2 "*Elect* according to the *foreknowledge* of God…"

One of the great proof-texts of Calvinism's Unconditional Election is Romans 8:28-30. This text is often misunderstood as being directed to unbelievers foreordained for salvation. However, the entire context proves that it is referring to people who are believers, who are already saved, who love God, whom God foreknew and predestined to be conformed to the image of His Son. The text simply does not say that God predetermines certain people to salvation and certain people to damnation based upon His sovereign choice. Instead, it shows that the general call of the gospel does result in justification and glorification of all whom God foreknew would believe.

Individual election in Scripture is always conditional, based on man's voluntary love and willing obedience. God, being eternal, ever-present and outside of the bounds of time, knows beforehand those who will be His and therefore their very names are *"written in the Book of Life from the foundation of the world"* [Revelation 17:8]. And those very names can just as easily be *"scratched out of the Book of Life"* (thus disproving their supposed Unconditional Election) if they depart from faith in Christ into spiritual death [Revelation 3:1-6; Exodus 32:33].

ISRAEL'S ELECTION AND INDIVIDUAL SALVATION

This same principle of "Conditional Election" is seen in God's gracious dealing with Israel in the Old Testament. God had chosen the nation of Israel, just as He has chosen the Church as a spiritual nation in Christ, solely by His love and sovereign choice [Deuteronomy 7:7-9; 9:5-7]. This truth was Paul's ultimate theological purpose for writing Romans 9-11. The nation of Israel was chosen by God *without condition* so that "the purpose of God according to election might stand, not of works but of Him who calls."

> Romans 9:10-13 "And not only this, but when Rebecca also had conceived by one man, even by our father Isaac (for the children not yet being born, nor having done any good or evil, that *the purpose of God according to election* might stand, not of works but of Him who calls), it was said to her, 'The older shall serve the younger.' As it is written, 'Jacob I have loved, but Esau I have hated.'"

> Isaiah 45:4 "…Israel My *elect*."

God, however, made a clear distinction between His sovereign choice of the nation and individual salvation. There was an unmistakable difference between Israel's corporate election as God's people - based upon God's sovereign grace, and personal salvation - based upon keeping the faith of Abraham. Rather than out to prove Calvinism's view of election, Paul was confirming that God had chosen His people (Israel/Jacob) not based upon works, but by grace. God put His sovereignty on display by choosing Israel as His special people out of every other nation, and He was not unjust in doing so!

> Romans 9:14 "What shall we say then? *Is there unrighteousness with God?* Certainly not!"

When Paul used the expression, *"Jacob have I loved, but Esau I have hated"* he was quoting from Malachi 1:2-5 which speaks of two individuals that represent two peoples (see Genesis 25:23). John Calvin himself said that these words *"refer to the whole progeny of the patriarch."*[41] Nowhere does this verse apply to all people in general whom God either loves or hates based on His sovereign decree. The text simply does not say that. Furthermore, it would make God unjust, and contradict what Paul has just stated about God being righteous in all that He does.

God's sovereignty allows Him to have mercy on whom He wants to have mercy, and harden whom He desires to harden. However, His justice keeps Him from doing that which is unrighteous. As an example, Paul referenced Pharaoh whom God showed mercy for a time yet hardened after Pharaoh repeatedly hardened his own heart to God [Exodus 7:13,22; 8:15,19,32; 9:7,12,34,35].

> Romans 9:15-18 "For He says to Moses, 'I will have mercy on whomever I will have mercy, and I will have compassion on whomever I will have compassion.' So then *it is not of him who wills, nor of him who runs, but of God who shows mercy.* For the Scripture says to Pharaoh, 'For this very purpose I have raised you up, that I may show My power in you, and that My name may be declared in all the earth.' Therefore *He has mercy on whom He wills, and whom He wills He hardens."*

For Calvinists, God chooses to harden most and show mercy to some for the sole purpose of making His power known. However, this view also makes Him wicked and unjust, which is the exact opposite intention of what Paul is communicating. It is important to remember that *Paul never connects Pharaoh's hardening by God with his salvation, nor the salvation of any other person for that matter.* Pharaoh was hardened so that God would display His glory in Israel's deliverance from Egypt – nothing more!

---

[41] John Calvin, *Institutes of the Christian Religion*, 3:21:7 (Peabody, Mass: Hendrickson Publishers, 2008), p. 612.

Paul's central point in writing Romans 9-11 is that God has chosen Israel as His special people, and who are we to question God's sovereign electing of the nation as the means by which He will bring salvation to the Gentiles? Despite the Calvinists' claim that Romans 9 is Paul's undisputed defense of Calvinism, Paul was defending the fact that Israel is still God's chosen people despite their present unbelief. God has not cast them away, nor has He replaced Israel with the Church. He is still at work among His people, and Paul himself is the chief example of this [Romans 11:1-6].

> Romans 11:2,5 *"God has not cast away His people* [Israel] *whom He foreknew... Even so then, at this present time there is a remnant according to the election of grace."*

Lest there be more confusion, Paul clarifies that God's choice of the nation does not guarantee that everyone who is a descendant of Israel will be saved. No one is saved because they are Jewish. They are accounted as righteous in God's sight because they believed just as Abraham and the fathers believed and were saved. Never was salvation in the Old Testament connected with keeping the works of the law, but by keeping the faith [Hebrews 11, Romans 4].

God ordained that membership of the elect nation be an issue of the outward circumcision of the flesh while individual salvation is an inward matter of circumcision of the heart, achieved only by grace through faith. Which is why Paul could say, *"They are not all Israel who are of Israel."* They are not all God's children simply because they are born Jewish. They are only God's children if their heart has been circumcised by Christ, in the Spirit, through faith.

> Romans 2:28-29 "For he is not a Jew who is one outwardly, nor is circumcision that which is outward in the flesh; but *he is a Jew who is one inwardly*; and circumcision is that of the heart, in the Spirit…"

> Romans 9:6-8 *"They are not all Israel who are of Israel*, nor are they all children because they are the seed of Abraham; but, 'In Isaac your seed shall be called.' That is, those who are the children of the flesh, these are not the children of God; *but the children of the promise are counted as the seed…"*

This distinction between God's sovereign decree of Israel's national election (which is unconditional) and individual election of members within the nation (which is conditional) is the foundation of the Arminian view of Conditional Election. God has chosen the Church, the corporate Body of Christ, in Him before the foundation of the world. This sovereign election is unconditional! God most certainly will have a people for Himself.

However, like Israel, personal salvation and participation into the elect nation (spiritually speaking) is conditional and achieved by grace through faith. Because of this God commands us to be diligent to make our call and election sure. We have a role, however small it may be, in God's electing purposes. If individual election were entirely God's sovereign choice (man having no responsibility or part in his salvation), there would be no need for us to make our "election sure." It also goes to say that it would be impossible for us to do this; for Calvinism says that God alone makes our election sure, not man.

> 2 Peter 1:10,11 "Brethren, *be even more diligent to make your call and election sure,* for if you do these things you will never stumble; for so an entrance will be supplied to you abundantly into the everlasting kingdom of our Lord and Savior Jesus Christ."

I understand that this simple explanation of election from Romans 9 is not sufficient for Calvinists. Nonetheless, we must be careful not to separate Chapter 9 from Chapters 10 and 11 as many often do. In his short work, *Killing Calvinism*, Calvinist Pastor Greg Dutcher quoted Paul's hymn of praise saying, "Oh, the depth of the riches and wisdom and knowledge of God! How unsearchable are His judgments and how inscrutable are His ways!" [Romans 11:33]. Then in typical Calvinist form, he goes on to say, "When Paul reflected on the doctrines that make up what we call Calvinism, he was moved to rejoice in God."[42]

As excellent as his book is (every Calvinist and non-Calvinist should read it), Pastor Greg misses the entire reason for Paul's rapturous moment of worship. Paul was not praising God for the doctrines of Calvinism, but rather for revealing the glorious mystery of God's plan to redeem rebellious Israel [Romans 11:25-32] through the instrumentality of the Church [Romans 11:11-24]. This simple mistake is no small matter and is the potential source of many other damaging theological errors (see Conclusion). Romans 9 does not stand alone. If we see the sovereignty of God in its full context, we can rejoice rightly in God, as prophetic voice Art Katz exclaims:

> "*What is Paul celebrating and what he is so rapturous about?* Evidently, Paul, in reviewing this great mystery, cannot contain himself any longer. He breaks out, 'Oh, the depth of the riches both of the wisdom and knowledge of God!' Something has broken upon his consciousness that even language strains to express. We need to ask ourselves, 'Why have we not become equally as rapturous?' Until we break forth in this kind of exclamation, we have not yet seen what Paul has seen... *Paul has caught a glimpse of the wisdom of God, not only with regard to Israel, but even more so with regard to the Church's relationship to Israel*, which is the only way to see the Church in its deepest and fullest identity." [43]

GOD IS A JUST JUDGE

Over and again the Bible tells us that God shows personal favoritism to no man and commands us to do the same [Galatians 2:6; James 2:1-9]. God is not divided against Himself. It would contradict His very nature

---

[42] Greg Dutcher, *Killing Calvinism* (Adelphi, MD: Cruciform Press, 2012), p. 18.
[43] Art Katz. *The Mystery of Israel and the Church*. Ebook. www.artkatzministries.org

and oppose His Word for Him to be partial to one by unconditionally electing an undeserving sinner while passing over and choosing not to elect another sinner just as undeserving. Our human understanding and definition of fairness does not matter when God has clearly defined it.

> Acts 10:34 "In truth I perceive that *God shows no partiality."*

> Romans 2:11 "For there is *no partiality with God."*

> Galatians 2:6 "God shows personal *favoritism to no man."*

> Deuteronomy 10:17 "For the LORD your God is God of gods and Lord of lords, the great God, mighty and awesome, who *shows no partiality* nor takes a bribe."

> 2 Chronicles 19:7 "…There is no iniquity with the LORD our God, *no partiality*, nor taking of bribes."

The Bible says that the Judge of all the earth shall do right and deal justly with men [Genesis 18:25]. God will not condemn a man or woman to an eternity of burning in the fires of hell for rejecting His gospel, when He made impossible for them to believe in the first place. If a human judge in our flawed court system acted that way, there would be rioting in the streets and shouts of "injustice" heard from miles away. Thankfully, God is not an unjust judge [Luke 18:1-8; Psalm 7:9-12].

God is certainly sovereign. But He is not evil, nor is He partial. He calls all men to Himself and gives them the opportunity to come to Him by faith. All who come to Him He will by no means cast out. Those who believe and are saved are His elect people, chosen for salvation, and redeemed by His blood!

"It's right for God to slaughter women and children anytime He pleases."

-John Piper

5

PROVIDENCE

The funeral was going well until the pastor, seeking to justify and explain the mystery of death said to the parents of a little boy, *"God's purpose is always greater than ours! This is why He took your child… He would rather him be with Jesus in heaven than with you on earth."* I have heard statements similar to these before, but never in real time and space, and that from a fellow man of God.

The questions were ringing through my head… Did God take their child? Why would He do that? And why would He want this precious little boy to be with Him in heaven than with his grieving family on earth? And even more puzzling, why in the world did this pastor feel the need to blame this terrible accident on God? Did he believe that God's meticulous providence had perfectly planned and ordained that this boy drown at that exact moment in time, in such a horrid manner, all for God's glory?

I do not know whether he was Calvinist or not. But I do know that such a view of the sovereignty of God is helpful to no one and clearly exceeds the jurisdiction of Scripture. Sometimes accidents happen. Life is hard. People make mistakes. And God is not responsible or to be blamed for everything in life that doesn't make sense, including every cancer diagnosis, terrorist attack, hurricane, McDonald's shooting spree, and accidental drowning.

Yes, God is sovereign, superintending over all of His creation. But neither is He the all-determining factor of every act of evil and crisis in the earth. The Biblical picture of the sovereignty of God says that no matter what happens in the world, for good or bad, there is a loving God, who, though He permits and allows sin and crisis, is still seated victorious on the throne. There, in that place, He is overseeing all things and working all things together for our good and His glory.

GOD'S SOVEREIGNTY AND MAN'S DIGNITY

Historically this expression of God's sovereignty has been called *Providence*. God's providence implies that He is King over His creation. He is active in the affairs of men and has the right to rule and reign over us with wisdom, kindness, and benevolence [Acts 17:24,25].

When the Bible speaks of God being sovereign, it is distinctly saying that we are not! We are not God! Nor is God made in our image. Only one is Supreme and Sovereign! And He is not us [Isaiah 45:5]. Who can read these verses and think otherwise?

> Psalm 115:3 "Our God is in heaven; *He does whatever He pleases*."
>
> Psalm 135:6 "*Whatever the LORD pleases He does*, in heaven and in earth…"
>
> Daniel 4:35 "All the inhabitants of the earth are reputed as nothing; *He does according to His will* in the army of heaven and among the inhabitants of the earth. *No one can restrain His hand* or say to Him, 'What have You done?'"

God is sovereign over all things, including everyone made in His image! Paul's climactic statement of the gospel to the Church in Rome was that "all things work together for good for those who love God and are called according to His purpose" [Romans 8:28]. God is not just supreme in some things but *all* things, because we are called to fulfill His sovereign purpose- not ours! It is *God who works* in us both to will and to do *for His good pleasure* [Philippians 2:13].

Intercessor E.M. Bounds writes of the sovereignty of God saying,

"God is everywhere, watching, superintending, overseeing, governing everything in the highest interest of man, and carrying forward His plans and executing His purposes in creation and redemption. *He is not an absentee God.* He did not make the world and all that is in it, and turn it over to so-called natural laws, and then retire into the secret places of the universe having no regard for it or for the working of His laws. His hand is on the throttle. The work is not beyond His control. *Earth's inhabitants and its affairs are not running independently of Almighty God.*"[44]

God's providence or sovereignty speaks not only of God's power and ability to do as He pleases, but also of His all-wise choice to rule over His creation with mankind made in His image. Scripture from Genesis to Revelation continually affirms that God has chosen to exercise His sovereign plan in the affairs of earth with those who are in submission to His rule.

At the start of creation, we discover that God chose to delegate the authority of the planet to man. Humanity was given a measure of power and dominion in the earth that other creatures were simply not given. Nowhere is this delegated authority to His saints more visible than in prayer, prophetic utterance, and partnering with God as He rules over creation.

> Genesis 1:26,28 "God said, 'Let Us make man in Our image, according to Our likeness; *let them have dominion…* over all the earth.' Then God blessed them, and God said to them, 'Be fruitful and multiply; fill the earth and subdue it; *have dominion….* over every living thing… on the earth.'"
>
> Psalm 115:16 "The heaven, even the heavens, are the LORD'S; But *the earth He has given to the children of men.*"

---

[44] E.M. Bounds, *The Complete Works of E.M. Bounds on Prayer* (Grand Rapids: Baker Books, 2004), p. 213.

> Psalm 8:4-6 "What is man that You are mindful of him, And the son of man that You visit him? …You have crowned him with glory and honor. *You have made him to have dominion over the works of Your hands*; You have put all things under his feet."

As an expression of man's dominion, we see that God chose to answer the prayers of weak and broken people. Even more significant is that many of these prayers changed and altered God's sovereign decrees. One minute God promised to send judgment and the next He turned away His wrath simply because someone prayed. God ordained that prayer uttered from the lips of human beings affect the will and work of God in the earth.

> Exodus 32:10-14 "'Now therefore, let Me alone, that My wrath may burn hot against them and I may consume them…' Then *Moses pleaded with the LORD his God… So the LORD relented* from the harm which *He said He would do* to His people."

> Jonah 3:1,4,5,10 "The word of the LORD came to Jonah… 'Yet *forty days, and Nineveh shall be overthrown*!' So the people of Nineveh believed God, proclaimed a fast, and put on sackcloth, from the greatest to the least of them… Then God saw their works, that they turned from their evil way; and *God relented from the disaster that He had said He would bring upon them*, and He did not do it."

We also find in the prophets that God chose to do nothing in the earth without first telling a prophetic voice what is in His heart. Almighty God, who can do what He wants, when He wants, however He wants, desired to include man and reveal His secrets to His servants before He did one thing on the earth. As the prophets spoke the mysteries of His heart, He then moved in response to their words [Ezekiel 37:1-7]. Time and time again in Scripture we see that without the Word of the Lord, the hand of the Lord never moved over creation [Genesis 1:3; Psalm 33:6].

> Amos 3:7 "Surely the Lord *GOD does nothing*, unless He reveals His secret to His servants the prophets."

Finally, as this age transitions to the age to come, we will see that God's desire is just as it was in the beginning as He rules and reigns on the earth with His people forever. Whatever your view is on the Millennium and New Heavens and New Earth, it is clear that God desires a future reign on the earth *with His saints* forever. We are going full-circle, back to Eden, back to the place where God and man rule over His creation in voluntary love and obedience.

> Daniel 7:27 "Then the kingdom and dominion, And *the greatness of the kingdoms under the whole heaven, Shall be given to the people*, the saints of the Most High."

> Revelation 20:6 "They [God's people] shall be priests of God and of Christ, and shall *reign with Him* a thousand years."

One cannot read these Scriptures and come to the conclusion that God's providential plan is somehow disconnected from His intimate relationship with His people. God loves man, uses man, and works with man to carry out His sovereign will. God, giving man freedom and dominion on the earth to bring forth change for the good or bad, does not insinuate that He is any less sovereign. Always, at all times He is still on the throne as the Almighty!

THE DANGER OF HYPER-SOVEREIGNTY

The providence of God is one of the most dynamic and life-changing truths of Scripture. It reminds us that in good times and bad, God is still God! We can take confidence in the fact that nothing catches Him by surprise. He knows what He is doing! He understands how to take a seemingly impossible and broken situation and turn it around for our ultimate good and His eternal glory.

However, over the years the subject of God's providence has been taken to an unbiblical extreme. This hyper-sovereignty often embraced and trumpeted by many Calvinists teaches that God is the secret source and divine instigator of all suffering, sin, sickness, evil, disease, death, poverty, depression, and every other negative thing that we have come to despise as humans. According to this view, sin and evil happen because God sovereignly decided long ago that it should.

One way or another God sees to it that all evil comes about yet, says the Calvinist, He is not responsible for causing any of it. He renders it certain and makes sure it happens down to the last detail yet He in no way is responsible for the actual evil itself. He sovereignly determines everything, decrees it, sets it in motion, and brings it forth based on His own will, but He is somehow not the one doing it. Calvinist author Craig Brown writes,

> "Although *God decrees evil*, He does not directly perform morally evil deeds… *Man is responsible* for his sin, not God." [45]

Consider Adam and Eve in the Garden of Eden. Calvinist's affirm that God planned and rendered their fall certain. Though God used secondary causes to bring sin into the world and fulfill His foreordained plan, they assert that God is not to be blamed for it. In this scenario one only wonders if Adam was actually given a choice to resist the forbidden tree and how God, who made their sin certain, is still considered innocent [Genesis 2:16,17]. As John Calvin acknowledged,

> "I freely acknowledge my doctrine to be this: *that Adam fell, not only by permission of God, but by His very secret counsel and decree*; and that Adam drew all his posterity with himself, by his fall, into eternal destruction." [46]

This scenario is much like the corrupt police officer who perfectly

---

[45] Craig R. Brown, *"The Five Dilemmas of Calvinism"* (Ligonier Ministries. Orlando, FL, 2007), reformedquotes.com
[46] John Calvin, *The Secret Providence of God* (1558). www.the-highway.com/Calvin2_section1.html.

arranges the crime scene, sets up the perpetrator to break a law that he had no possible way of avoiding, and then feels justified (and glorified if you're a Calvinist) in arresting and sending him to prison for a multiple-term life sentence. In the same manner, Calvinism says that God decreed and made all sin certain according to His secret counsel; yet He finds pleasure in damning unbelievers to hell for a crime they had no choice to commit.

According to Calvinism, the fallen creature is always responsible for all sin and evil they enact. Therefore God is just in judging them and sending them to hell forever; though He made sure, by His sovereign will and decree, they would act out the evil in the first place and gave them no choice to do otherwise. Are you confused yet? Don't worry! So is every other believer who first hears the hyper-sovereignty fueled by Reformed Theology.

Think for a moment of Calvinism's view of Unconditional Election. The very God who calls every sinner on the earth to repent [Acts 17:30], has already foreordained and determined most to be damned. Some are saved because God decided to show them grace, and the rest are doomed because God has determined to pass them over and leave them in their sins. God somehow calls them to repent and pleads with them to repent, though He has sovereignly decreed and determined that they not repent.

God offers sinners something He never intended to give and is somehow glorified in their everlasting burnings. To soften the blow of such a dreadful decree Calvinists rarely focus on the negative implications of Calvinism but emphasize the positive and gracious act of God in choosing to elect a sinner like me!

> "The sufficient answer to all the wicked accusations that the doctrine of Predestination is cruel, horrible, and unjust, is that, unless God had chosen certain ones to salvation, none would have been saved."[47]

A.W. Pink's statement above is characteristic of Calvinists, yet it

---

[47] A.W. Pink, *The Sovereignty of God* (Edinburg: The Banner of Truth Trust, 1961), p. 239.

does not lessen the severity of hyper-sovereignty when applied to those who are not included in the "special group" of the elect. Pink is right in saying that Calvinism's doctrine of election is cruel, horrible, and unjust. Such wicked accusations are more than accusations; they are true. Calvin himself acknowledged, "The decree (i.e., God's choice to damn billions just because He is God and can do so) is *dreadful indeed*, I confess."[48]

Just like his brother John, Arminian hymn writer Charles Wesley was so grieved over this dangerous doctrine that he boldly wrote worship hymns to confront it:

> "Ah! Gentle, gracious Dove,
> And art thou grieved in me,
> That sinners should restrain thy love,
> And say, 'It is not free:
> It is not free for all:
> The most, thou passest by,
> And mockest with a fruitless call
> Whom *thou hast doom'd to die.*'
>
> O HORRIBLE DECREE
> Worthy of whence it came!
> Forgive their hellish blasphemy
> Who charge it on the Lamb:
> Whose pity him inclin'd
> To leave his throne above,
> The friend, and Saviour of mankind,
> The God of grace, and love.
>
> O gracious, loving Lord,
> I feel thy bowels yearn;
> For those who slight the gospel word
> I share in thy concern:

---

[48] John Calvin, *Institutes of the Christian Religion*, 3:23:7 (Peabody, Mass: Hendrickson Publishers, 2008), p. 630.

How art thou grieved to be
By ransom'd worms withstood!
How dost thou bleed afresh to see
Them trample on thy blood!

Sinners, abhor the fiend:
His other gospel hear—
The God of truth did not intend
The thing his words declare,
He offers grace to all,
Which most cannot embrace,
Mocked with an ineffectual call
And insufficient grace.

The righteous God consigned
Them over to their doom,
And sent the Saviour of mankind
To *damn them from the womb*;
To damn for falling short,
Of *what they could not do*,
For not believing the report
Of that which was not true.

The *God of love pass'd by*
The most of those that fell,
Ordain'd poor reprobates to die,
And forced them into hell.
'He did not do the deed'
(Some have more mildly rav'd)
He did not damn them—but decreed
They never should be saved.

He did not them bereave
Of life, or stop their breath,

His grace he only would not give,
And starv'ed their souls to death.
Satanic sophistry!
But still, all-gracious God,
They charge the sinner's death on thee,
Who bought'st him with thy blood.

How long, O God, how long
Shall Satan's rage proceed!
Wilt thou not soon avenge the wrong,
And crush the serpent's head?
Surely thou shalt at last
Bruise him beneath our feet:
*The devil and his doctrine cast
Into the burning pit.*

Arise, O God, arise,
Thy glorious truth maintain,
Hold forth the bloody sacrifice,
For every sinner slain!
Defend thy mercy's cause,
Thy grace divinely free,
Lift up the standard of thy cross,
Draw all men unto thee.

My life I here present,
My heart's last drop of blood,
O let it all be freely spent
In proof that thou art good,
Art good to all that breathe,
Who all may pardon have:
Thou willest not the sinner's death,
But all the world wouldst save.

> O take me at my word,
> But arm me with thy power,
> Then call me forth to suffer, Lord,
> To meet the fiery hour:
> In death will I proclaim
> That all may hear thy call,
> And clap my hands amidst the flame,
> And shout —*'HE DIED FOR ALL.'*"[49]

GOD IN THE IMAGE OF SATAN

For the Calvinist, hyper-sovereignty extends far beyond salvation and election. It also applies to everything that happens in life, whether it is good or evil. God's providence, according to Calvinism, declares that God Himself is the sovereign orchestrator behind all things including every work of sin and darkness. As Calvinist scholar Edwin Palmer writes, *"All things, including sin, are brought to pass by God."*[50]

Imagine coming home to find your spouse and four children brutally raped and stabbed to death by a murderous sociopath. Did God cause this to happen? The true Calvinist would say that God rendered it certain and determined that it would take place for His glory though He did not commit the evil. God, in this sense, is the Uncaused Cause behind everything that happens including the very things that His Word declares He hates such as murder and rape.

We must ask ourselves these questions: Did God will and ordain that the famous football coach Jerry Sandusky sexually abuse multitudes of innocent young boys for untold years, all for His glory? Did God will and ordain that a troubled young man shoot and kill twenty students and six teachers at Sandy Hook Elementary School, all for His glory? Did God will and ordain that six men in Delhi, India brutally rape and kill a twenty-three-year-old student on a bus, all for His glory?

---

[49] Charles Wesley, Hymn: *"Oh Horrible Decree,"* taken in part by the author.
[50] Edwin Palmer, *Five Points of Calvinism*, p 101.

Is this the Biblical picture of God's sovereignty? Is it true that nothing happens in life that is outside of God's ordained, predetermined will? Consider again the words of John Piper.

> "In some way (that we may not be able to fully comprehend) God is able without blameworthy 'tempting' *to see to it* that a person does what God ordains for him to do *even if it involves evil.*"[51]

The reason Piper included in parenthesis the phrase "that we may not be able to fully comprehend" is because he is well aware that this reasoning is utterly confusing and mind boggling. I often scratch my head when Calvinists speak of God's *causing all events* to happen according to His predetermined plan, yet cling to the Scriptures that speak of God not being the author of sin and evil. Somehow God (as in the case of Sandy Hook) wills murder, plans murder, orchestrates murder, and renders murder certain, but yet He is not the author of murder.

Scripture does maintain that there are times where God acts in judgment in response to the sin of man. In unique cases throughout the Old and New Testament, we find that God does bring about sickness, destruction, or even death as an act of His judgment [Acts 5:1-11].

> Isaiah 45:7 "I form the light and create darkness, I make peace and *create calamity*; I, the LORD, do all these things."

> Revelation 2:21-23 "I gave her time to repent of her sexual immorality, and she did not repent. Indeed *I will cast her into a sickbed*, and those who commit adultery with her into great tribulation, unless they repent of their deeds. *I will kill her children with death*, and all the churches shall know that I am He who searches the minds and hearts."

---

[51] John Piper, *Still Sovereign: Contemporary Perspectives on Election, Foreknowledge, and Grace* (Grand Rapids: Baker, 2000), p. 123.

> 1 Corinthians 11:29-32 "For he who eats and drinks in an unworthy manner eats and drinks *judgment* to himself, not discerning the Lord's body. For this reason *many are weak and sick among you*, and many die. For if we would judge ourselves, we would not be judged. But *when we are judged, we are chastened by the Lord*, that we may not be condemned with the world."

These verses are valid and relevant for today, but we must not quickly assume that because God acts in judgment at unique times and unique ways that He is the divine cause or sovereign orchestrator behind every evil, sin, or sickness that takes place in the world. Scripture simply does not affirm this. If that be the case, there is ultimately nothing for the Devil to do or scheme, for God has replaced him and He being sovereign does Satan's job far better.

The critical issue at hand isn't whether or not God *permits* sin and evil actions from men but whether He *ordains* all of it as His perfect sovereign plan. If you believe in Calvinism's portrait of God's meticulous providence in all things, be sure that you will be forced to embrace a God who is immoral, unholy, and at the end of the day unworthy of worship.

In his book *"The Doors of the Sea: Where Was God in the Tsunami?,"* David Bentley Hart hammered home this truth saying, "If indeed there were a God whose true nature- whose justice or sovereignty- were revealed in the death of a child or the dereliction of a soul or a predestined hell, then *it would be no great transgression to think of him as a kind or malevolent or contemptible demiurge* [i.e., a wicked and loathsome orchestrator of evil], and to hate him, and to deny him worship, and to seek a better God than he."[52]

It is not hard to see why the non-Calvinists' stomach churns when they hear such a portrait of God. It contradicts the very nature of Him as He has revealed so plainly in His Word. When God's love and kindness toward men are de-emphasized or rejected for an extreme, unbiblical view of God's sovereignty, God's very image is marred. He no longer looks like God, but Satan. The two become indistinguishable in their

---

[52] David Bentley Hart, *The Doors of the Sea* (Grand Rapids: Eerdmans, 2005), p. 91.

plans, purposes, and intentions.

Whether Calvinist or not, the believer who confuses the simple truth of John 10:10, has fallen into dangerous theological territory. In all things and at all times, even times of judgment, we must remember that Jesus Christ has come to give us life and life more abundantly. Never does He steal, kill and destroy; and never will God assume the role of Satan for some mysterious "greater good" of His glory.

> John 10:10 "The thief does not come except to steal, and to kill, and to destroy. *I have come that they may have life*, and that they may have it more abundantly."

PROVIDENCE AND FREE WILL

Like Calvinists, Arminians rejoice in the providence of God, though they view them very differently. But unlike Calvinists, they also recognize that God in His sovereignty has chosen to limit Himself. God is on the throne, but He has given man the dignity of making real decisions that have real eternal outcomes, without God having to manipulate the circumstances to see that they happen.

A.W. Tozer describes the Arminian view of God's providence when he says,

> "God sovereignly decreed that man should be free to exercise moral choice, and man from the beginning has fulfilled that decree by making his choice between good and evil. When he chooses to do evil, he does not thereby countervail the sovereign will of God but fulfills it, inasmuch as *the eternal decree decided not which choice the man should make but that he should be free to make it*. If in His absolute freedom God has willed to give man limited freedom, who is there to stay His hand or say, 'What doest thou?' *Man's will is free because God is sovereign.* A God less than sovereign could not bestow moral freedom upon His creatures. He would

be afraid to do so."[53]

From the beginning, God created man with free will. Man was free to make choices for good or evil, which is why He placed one tree in the garden forbidden for mankind to eat. God desired relationship that was not coerced. Sadly, Adam and Eve chose to disobey God and eat the fruit. Nowhere do we find that God decreed the fall to happen, nor are we to conclude that God was ultimately responsible for their decision. They wanted to sin, and God gave them over to their request.

The Bible tells us that man is in a constant place of tension before God. He is free to make choices for good or evil, and he is rewarded or judged based upon those decisions [Leviticus 26:21; Deuteronomy 30:19; Joshua 24:15; John 5:40]. Through all this, God is still sovereign, in control, overseeing and seeing to it that His perfect will is brought forth in real time and space. God's sovereignty and man's freedom work together in perfect harmony.

> "An ocean liner leaves New York bound for Liverpool. Its destination has been determined by proper authorities. *Nothing can change it...* On board the liner are several scores of passengers. *These are not in chains, neither are their activities determined for them by decree.* They are completely free to move about on the deck, read, talk, altogether as they please, but all the while the great liner is carrying them steadily onward toward a predetermined point.
>
> *Both freedom and sovereignty are present here and they do not contradict each other.* So it is, I believe, with man's freedom and the sovereignty of God. The mighty liner of God's sovereign design keeps its steady course over the sea of history. God moves undisturbed and unhindered toward the fulfillment of those eternal purposes which He purposed in Christ Jesus before the world began."[54]

---

[53] A.W. Tozer, *The Knowledge of the Holy* (New York, NY: HarperOne, 1961), p. 110-111.
[54] Ibid. p. 111.

To summarize Tozer, God orchestrates His sovereign plan without turning man into robots and undermining the freedom that He has given us. Such is the case with Joseph in the Old Testament and Jesus in the New. God foreknew the decisions of Joseph's brothers and worked his plan of deliverance for Israel through them without having to pull their puppet strings. Thus, Joseph could affirm that God's providence was working through these events though his brothers meant it for evil.

> Genesis 45:5 "*God sent me* before you to preserve life."

> Genesis 50:20 "You meant evil against me; but *God meant it for good…*"

Consider the case of Christ. God used Herod and Pilate, and through them orchestrated the death of Jesus on the cross without needing to control their every decision and violate their free will. In His providence, God worked His perfect eternal plan through them. It happened just as God planned it would be done and Jesus was delivered up to the cross by the determined purpose and foreknowledge of God.

> Acts 2:23 "Him, being delivered by the *determined purpose and foreknowledge of God*, you have taken by lawless hands, have crucified, and put to death."

> Acts 4:27,28 "Against Your holy Servant Jesus, whom You anointed, both Herod and Pontius Pilate, with the Gentiles and the people of Israel, were gathered together *to do whatever Your hand and Your purpose determined before to be done.*"

I understand that Calvinists will undoubtedly press how God could work through all sorts of scenarios to bring forth His perfect plan. However, this is not difficult when we consider that our God is all-knowing and all-wise. God is in control and He is very, very smart. We do not have to create a God who micromanages the world just to get what He wants. God is sovereign and He knows what He is doing.

When our vision of God's sovereignty mars His image and makes Him a wicked tyrant, we must think again whether or not our "sovereign God" is the God of the Bible! God is the one who has ordained that man exercise free moral choice whether it is for good or bad, for salvation or damnation. To say otherwise is to make Him a moral monster who is not a loving, merciful, beautiful, gracious God.

God's love compels Him to give man freedom to choose. He is not intimidated by our freedom. He is not worried that our ability to choose somehow makes Him less than who He is and that it somehow makes us like God. Our freedom is only by His will and His plan for our good and His glory. Sovereign freedom given to man is the fruit of God's desire for joyful relationship, not coerced obedience.

The statement of the cross is the providence of God put on full display over the history of man. The sovereign, redemptive purpose of God reached its climax when God sent His Son to die for the sins of the world, that through Him all might be saved [John 1:29; 3:16,17; 4:42; Romans 5:8,9; 1 Timothy 1:16; 2 Peter 3:9].

Despite our many efforts to trample on the very freedom He has given us by choosing sin; He has brought forth His plan, won us over, and called forth a bride from every tribe, kindred and tongue. His saints are not those who were forced to the wedding [Matthew 22:1-14]. They have willingly and joyfully surrendered to the Son by grace alone, through faith alone, by love alone, for the glory of God alone.

"Sinners do not limit the atonement, God does."

-John MacArthur

6

ATONEMENT

God desires *all* men to be saved and come to the knowledge of the truth [1 Timothy 2:3,4]. Period. End of story! No matter what else we may believe concerning the scope and effectiveness of Jesus' atonement, we must begin here. Jesus loves all men and longs for the salvation of all men! He came, He died, and He rose again three days later for this purpose. Any other teaching contrary to this foundational gospel truth is a lie against the One who has already spoken.

What Jesus has accomplished through His death on the cross is no small matter. It is the single most crucial aspect of the gospel and is what makes the good news good news. Jesus freely shed His blood for your sin and my sin. He died for the sins of men [John 1:29, 1 Peter 1:19]. The song of the ages sung by saints and angels alike will forever extol the glory of Christ's atonement in redeeming men to God by His blood.

> Revelation 5:9 "You are worthy to take the scroll, And to open its seals; for You were slain, and have *redeemed us to God by Your blood out* of every tribe and tongue and people and nation."

The cross is the ultimate statement of Christ fully and finally bridging the gap of a fallen world and a holy God. In Himself, He brought God to man and man to God, having made peace through the blood of His cross. He accomplished redemption once and for all [Hebrews 7:27; 9:12; 10:10]. Jesus forever made a way by which undeserving sinners can come to Him through the riches of His extravagant grace.

> 2 Corinthians 5:19 "God was in Christ *reconciling the world to Himself,* not imputing their trespasses to them, and has committed to us the word of reconciliation."

The atonement begins with the fact that God was working in and through Christ to reconcile the world to Himself. The Father made two parties that were opposed "at one" through His Son (i.e., at-one-ment). Sinful humanity that was once cut off from God by sin has graciously been provided a way of salvation. Now we can come boldly to the Father through Jesus without shame, condemnation or fear of rejection.

In describing the atonement scholar John Stott defined it as, "An action by which *two conflicting parts are made 'at one'* or the state in which their oneness is enjoyed and expressed. This 'atonement,' Paul says, we have 'received' through our Lord and Saviour Jesus Christ. We have not ourselves achieved it by our own effort; we have received it from Him as a gift. *Sin caused an estrangement; the cross, the crucifixion of Christ, has accomplished an atonement.*"[55]

We could not redeem and ransom ourselves. It was too high a price. As the anonymous quote goes, "Jesus came to pay a debt He did not owe because we owed a debt we could not pay." Only one who was without sin, fully God and fully man could perfectly pay for man's transgression and freely justify the one who puts faith in Jesus. As a propitiation for sin, Jesus Christ became the sinless sacrifice that bore the wrath of God that we rightfully deserved. Jesus atoned for our sins and was willingly punished in our place to demonstrate God's love and satisfy God's justice.

> Romans 3:23-26 "*All have sinned...* being justified freely by His grace through the redemption that is in Christ Jesus, whom God set forth as a *propitiation* by His blood, through faith, to

---

[55] Stott, John. *Basic Christianity* (Downers Grove, IL: Inter-Varsity Press, 1971), p. 82.

demonstrate His righteousness… that He might be just and the justifier of the one who has faith in Jesus."

The Biblical picture of the atonement is called *Penal Substitution*. Jesus did not merely die *for* others but in the place of others. He died our death that we might share in His life. Jesus substituted Himself in our place that we might be saved from the wrath of God through the blood of His Son.

> Isaiah 53:6 "All we like sheep have gone astray; we have turned, every one, to his own way; and *the LORD has laid on Him the iniquity of us all.*"

> 2 Corinthians 5:21 "He made Him who knew no sin *to be sin for us*, that we might become the righteousness of God in Him."

As simple as this seems, this is where the debate over the atonement begins. Most Calvinists and Arminians believe that Jesus died for our sins, took our punishment, and substituted Himself in our place that we might be reconciled to God. But both disagree entirely on the nature and extent of the atoning work of Jesus at the cross.

The cross is the crux of the gospel, and more than any other truth we must get this one thing right. If we misunderstand what Jesus accomplished through His death and misconstrue who He came to save, we have another gospel. It is not good news for the entire world, as the Bible says [John 3:16]. It is terrible news for most and excellent news for some. And if the gospel is not good news for all, it is a lie straight from the depths of hell.

THE UNIVERSAL SCOPE OF THE GOSPEL

The difference between Calvinists and non-Calvinists on the truth of the atonement is worlds apart. Calvinists say the atonement is limited to and only efficient for the unconditionally elect. Non-Calvinists, and most Christians who are avid readers of the Bible, say it is available to all people and sufficient to save all who believe. But which view is right? Scripture tells us the answer in simple and straightforward terms:

- God, our Savior, desires *all* men to be saved and know the truth.

    1 Timothy 2:3,4 "God our Savior… *desires all men to be saved and to come to the knowledge of the truth.*"

- God longs that none would perish but that *all* come to repentance.

    2 Peter 3:9 "The Lord is not slack concerning His promise, as some count slackness, but is longsuffering toward us, *not willing that any should perish* but that *all should come to repentance.*"

- Jesus was lifted up on the cross so that *all* peoples would be drawn to Him.

    John 12:32 "And I, if I am lifted up from the earth, will *draw all peoples to Myself.*"

- He draws all men because He died for *all*.

    2 Corinthians 5:15 "*He died for all*, that those who live should live no longer for themselves, but for Him who died for them and rose again."

- Now, through Him, the gift of salvation came to *all* men.

    Romans 5:18 "Through one Man's righteous act *the free gift came to all men*, resulting in justification of life."

- And God's grace that brings salvation has been revealed to *all* men.

Titus 2:11 "For the grace of God that brings salvation has appeared to *all men.*"

- Therefore, God commands *all* men everywhere to repent. (Obviously, God would not command and expect us to do something that He foreordained us not to do.)

    Acts 17:30 "Truly, these times of ignorance God overlooked, but now commands *all men everywhere to repent.*"

- And to His glory, *all* who call upon Jesus for salvation will be saved.

    Romans 10:12,13 "The same Lord over all is rich to *all who call upon Him.* For '*whoever* calls on the name of the LORD *shall be saved.*'"

It is difficult to read these verses and assume that Jesus did not come for all, or that salvation (the means of grace accomplished at the cross) is ultimately not available to all men. God's desire, the deep longing of His heart, is that *no one* would perish, but all would be saved and come to repentance. In a crowd of ten thousand unbelievers, there is not one that Jesus doesn't ache over and long to be eternally saved. The salvation of the souls of *all men* is the burden of His heart, and it should be the burden of ours [Ezekiel 33:11].

However, we know from the testimony of Scripture that not all men will be saved! He draws all men, calls all men, and gives grace to all men for salvation, but not all will respond in repentance and faith. The way to life is narrow and difficult, and few find it [Matthew 7:13,14]. Many are called, but few are chosen [Matthew 22:13,14]. Some will forever inherit the Kingdom, and some will forever be cast into hell [Matthew 25:46].

There is no biblical Universalism. It is either Heaven or Hell, eternal bliss or eternal destruction. And let me add that men do not send themselves to hell, but God sends them there for their willful rebellion and sin. He is the only one who has the power to cast into hell and will be perfectly just and right in doing so [Luke 12:5].

JESUS DID NOT DIE FOR ALL MEN?

Interestingly, at its heart, Calvinism teaches that Jesus did not die for all men, but only the elect. This is the Achilles Heel of Calvinism and the most troubling point in TULIP theology. Many Calvinists themselves run from it like the plague, becoming "Four Point Calvinists" rather than five, yet it makes no difference whether one believes in it or not as long as one holds fast to Unconditional Election. If God has *not* chosen some to be saved from the foundation of the earth who even cares whether or not Christ has died for them?

Five Point Calvinism denies the universal scope of the atonement and declares it to be only effective for the unconditionally elect. It is not too strong to say that Calvinism disagrees with most of the Biblical texts written above. According to Calvinism,

- Jesus does *not* desire *all* men to be saved, but only desires the salvation of the elect.

- He does *not* will that *all* come to repentance, but only wills the repentance of the elect.

- He is *not* drawing *all* peoples to Himself, but only is effectually drawing the elect.

- He did *not* die for *all*, but only for the elect.

- The free gift of salvation is *not* available to *all*, but is only available to the elect.

- God's saving grace has *not* appeared to *all* men, but only irresistibly to the elect.

- God does *not* command *all* men everywhere to repent, for all men can't repent unless they are elect and foreordained to repent.

- *All* who call upon Him for salvation will *not* be saved, but only the elect that calls upon Him.

John Piper affirms this by saying,

> "…the death of Christ was designed for the salvation of God's people, *not for every individual.*"[56]

As does John Owen, one of the leading Calvinists of all time,

> "The Scripture *nowhere* saith Christ died *for all men.*"[57]

And the Canons of Dort,

> "For this was the sovereign counsel, and the most gracious will and purpose of God the Father, that the quickening and saving efficacy of *the most precious death of his Son should extend to all the elect*, for bestowing *upon them alone* the gift of justifying faith, thereby to bring them infallibly to salvation."[58]

Along with the Westminster Confession of Faith,

> "The Lord Jesus, by his perfect obedience, and sacrifice of himself, which he, through the eternal Spirit, once offered up

---

[56] John Piper, *TULIP: What We Believe about the Five Points of Calvinism* (Minneapolis, Minn.: Desiring God Ministries, 1997), www.desiringgod.org.
[57] John Owen. *"The Death of Christ, Volume 10 of the Works of John Owen."* Ed. By William H. Goold (Edinburgh: The Banner of Truth Trust, 1967), p. 245.
[58] Canons of Dort, II:8

unto God, hath fully satisfied the justice of his Father; and purchased, not only reconciliation, but an everlasting inheritance in the kingdom of heaven, *for all those whom the Father hath given unto Him.*"[59]

This doctrine is the "L" in TULIP called *Limited Atonement* or *Particular Redemption*. In short, it teaches that the atoning work of Jesus on the cross is *sufficient* for all, but is *limited* to those whom God has already chosen to be saved. What Jesus accomplished on the cross is limited to a particular group of people – the elect!

Calvinism says that God never wanted or intended to save those who were not elect and therefore Christ's blood was never shed for them. He only made a "Limited Atonement" for those whom He foreordained to be saved. Again this point of TULIP is pointless and unnecessary when we consider the ramifications of Unconditional Election. If God has already decided who to save, the non-elect will still go to hell regardless of whether Christ died for them or not.

To counteract this argument and make such a repugnant doctrine more palatable, Calvinists often focus on the extent of Christ's death as being "efficacious" only for God's people. John Piper declares that if you believe that God died for all men, you would therefore "believe that the death of Christ did not actually save anybody; it only made all men savable."[60] He goes on to say, "If Christ died for all men in the same way then He did not purchase regenerating grace for those who are saved."[61]

Piper is affirming that for the entire Calvinist system to work (i.e., God irresistibly drawing the elect and regenerating them without their repentance or faith because of their supposed Unconditional Election); one has to believe that the atonement is limited only to a select few chosen by a sovereign God. This philosophical argument in defense of Calvinism does not change the fact that Calvinists repudiate that Jesus died for all men and truly wants all of them to be saved [2 Corinthians

---

[59] Westminster Confession, VIII:5.
[60] John Piper, *TULIP: What We Believe about the Five Points of Calvinism* (Minneapolis, Minn.: Desiring God Ministries, 1997), www.desiringgod.org.
[61] Ibid.

5:15; 1 Timothy 2:3,4; Acts 17:30]. [62]

Like other Calvinists, Piper then flips the script and falsely accuses Arminians of limiting the atonement because they do not believe the nature of the atonement as including coerced regeneration or salvation. I find this sad and somewhat amusing because it is the Calvinists themselves who emphatically teach "Limited Atonement" – not Arminians.

> "It is not the Calvinist who limits the atonement. It is the Arminian… *The Arminian limits the nature and value and effectiveness of the atonement…* to a powerless opportunity for men to save themselves from their terrible plight of depravity."[63]

Seriously? Because we believe that the death of Christ is offered to all men as Scripture plainly declares, yet deny that the nature of the atonement includes the other unbiblical facets of Calvinism, we are the ones who are now limiting it? This misrepresentation is characteristic of many Calvinists who falsely accuse Arminians of restricting the power of the atonement in an attempt to remove the focus off its abhorrent claim that Jesus never shed His blood, nor intended to save all men.

QUENCHING CHRIST'S ATONEMENT

It will be helpful to clarify the Arminian position of the scope and nature of the atonement so that it does not become distorted and defined as something it is not. Despite what Piper says Arminians do not embrace a view of the atonement that believes that men can save themselves from their terrible depravity by their own free will. No devoted Arminian would ever espouse such a view.

Arminians believe that the atonement of Christ is both *sufficient* and *available* to all who respond in repentance and faith, though they

---

[62] Some dare to claim that He still somehow want all to be saved in a "secret" way, yet their very grip on Limited Atonement contradicts them.
[63] Ibid.

emphatically affirm that not all will be saved. If Jesus died for all, as Scripture plainly says, He, therefore, made atonement for the sins of the world. Jesus bore God's wrath for the sins of all men so that all through Him might be saved.

> 1 John 2:2 "He Himself is the *propitiation* for *our sins*, and not for ours only but *also for the whole world*."

> Hebrews 2:9 "…He [Jesus], by the grace of God, might *taste death for everyone*."

Salvation is not limited to those whom God has sovereignly chosen in a heavenly lottery, but is available to all who respond to God's prevenient grace, which is why He is calling and drawing all men to Himself. Neither Jacob Arminius, nor John Wesley concocted such an idea. It is clear in Scripture. God would not call men, draw men, and command all men to repent if He never intended that they ever receive the saving benefits of the cross. The scope of the atonement is undoubtedly for all men!

As Article 2 of the Arminian Remonstrance affirms,

> "Indeed, it is Christ's *unlimited atonement* that serves as the necessary foundation of *the genuine offer of salvation held out to all in the gospel* and is in accord with the command to preach the gospel to all."

Confusion on this subject will abound unless we see that there is an unmistakable difference between the *availability* of the atonement which is universal and the *application* of the atonement which is individual. The benefits of the cross are not made effective in someone's life merely because Jesus died. They must *apply* the blood of the slain Lamb over their life through repentance and faith. In like manner of Israel's Passover in the Old Testament, the death of the Lamb itself saved no one until it was actually applied by faith [Exodus 12:21,22; 1 Corinthians

5:7].

    The atonement is only made effectual when one responds to God's call through faith. Despite what Calvinists teach, no Scripture affirms that Christ saved all of the elect the moment that Jesus died on Calvary's tree. Instead, Calvary is what made salvation obtainable to all men because Jesus bore the sins of all [Isaiah 53:6].

    Limited Atonement says that God has a select group of people who are *saved already*, the moment that Jesus died, though they may not yet know it. All believers were in a sense saved before they were born because of their Unconditional Election and effectual atonement. However, Scripture testifies to the exact opposite. Namely, that all men are "condemned already" because they have not believed in the Son of God.

> John 3:17,18 "For God did not send His Son into the world to condemn the world, but that *the world through Him might be saved. He who believes in Him is not condemned, but he who does not believe is condemned already* because he has not believed in the name of the only begotten Son of God."

    Christ's unlimited atonement does not rob God of His glory or promote Christian Universalism. This truth is not incompatible with the fact that many will be cast into the lake of fire forever because they rejected His gospel. However difficult this tension may seem; it is not answered by absolving man of his responsibility and blaming God for limiting the cross only to a select few.

LIMITED OR UNLIMITED ATONEMENT?

Calvinists often point to various Scriptures to reinforce their belief that Jesus did not die for all men but only the elect. In an attempt to distract from the negative implications of Limited Atonement, Calvinists reference assorted proof-texts to back up this claim. But does Scripture plainly contradict itself and override the other texts that emphatically state that Jesus died for *all*?

First, consider Matthew 1:21. Calvinists focus on that fact that it says "He will save *His people* from their sins." However, the precise context of this verse speaks of Christ first and foremost bringing salvation to His very own people- the people of Israel. Nowhere in this passage, or in all of the Gospels, does Jesus exclude sinful men from possibility of salvation and limit the atonement to the "elect."

> Matthew 1:21 "He will *save His people* from their sins."

> Luke 1:77 "To give knowledge of *salvation to His people* by the remission of their sins…"

Second, consider John 10:15. Calvinists highlight that Christ as the good shepherd "gives His life for *the sheep*." While they put emphasis on the exclusivity of the sheep, we find that in the very same text, Jesus affirms that His sheep who find pasture specifically refers to "anyone" who enters by Him and is saved. Nowhere do we find Jesus limiting the potential of the cross to a random, chosen group who are special recipients of sovereign grace.

> John 10:9-15 "I am the door. If *anyone* enters by Me, he will be saved, and will go in and out and *find pasture*… I am the good shepherd. The good shepherd gives His life *for the sheep*… I lay down My life *for the sheep*."

Third, consider Matthew 20:28. Calvinists draw attention to the language that Jesus died as a "*ransom for many*" as undeniable proof of Limited Atonement. However, many ignore the corresponding Scripture that says Christ gave Himself as a ransom *for all*. Scripture never refers to Jesus as the mediator between God and the elect alone. He is the mediator between God and men, and therefore He gave Himself as a ransom for all!

Matthew 20:28 "The Son of Man did not come to be served, but to serve, and to give His life a *ransom for many*."

1 Timothy 2:5,6 "For there is one God and one Mediator between God and men, the Man Christ Jesus, who gave Himself a *ransom for all…*"

Like every other text to prove Limited Atonement, these verses fail to establish that salvation is ultimately not available for everyone and that Christ only died for the elect. Remember the simplicity of Paul's exegesis on the extent of the atonement: "He died for *all*" [2 Corinthians 5:15]. In fact, Scripture gives even more incriminating evidence against Limited Atonement when it also declares that Christ died and paid for the salvation of those who will eventually perish [Hebrews 10:29].

Romans 14:15 "Do not *destroy* with your food *the one for whom Christ died*."

2 Peter 2:1 "There will be false teachers among you, who will secretly bring in destructive heresies, even *denying the Lord who bought them*, and bring on themselves swift *destruction*."

John the Apostle makes a sweeping statement when he declared that "Jesus Christ is the propitiation for our sins, and not ours only, but also *for the whole world*" [1 John 2:2]. Jesus' wrath bearing sacrifice was sufficient for our sins and the sins of all men. It is not reserved for the elect but available to all who repent and believe. Jesus is the Savior and sin-bearer of the world!

1 John 4:14 "The Father has sent the Son as *Savior of the world*."

John 12:47 "I did not come to judge the world but to *save the world*."

> 2 Corinthians 5:19 "God was in Christ *reconciling the world* to Himself."
>
> John 1:29 "Behold! The Lamb of God who takes away the *sin of the world!*"
>
> John 4:42 "This is indeed the Christ, the *Savior of the world.*"

The doctrine of Particular Redemption does not like the word "world" and must (in many cases) redefine its meaning to refer to the "elect." As John Piper writes, "The 'whole world' *refers to the children of God scattered throughout the whole world.*"[64] Sadly, this completely twists what Scripture actually says all for the sake of defending Limited Atonement.

Clearly, the Greek word for world *'kosmos'* in Scripture never refers to the elect but includes both the saved and unsaved for whom Christ came [John 1:10; 3:16, 17; 7:7; 8:23; 13:1; 14:17,19; 15:18; 17:6, 9, 14, 25].

> John 3:16,17 "For *God so loved the world* that He gave His only begotten Son, that *whoever* believes in Him should not perish but have everlasting life. For God did not send His Son into the world to condemn the world, but *that the world through Him might be saved.*"

Does God truly love the world as Jesus says, or does He only like the elect and irresistibly draw them while leaving everyone else condemned to hell for His glory? Does He want the world to be saved or does He not? Calvinism says NO! Arminianism says YES! God loves the world and sent His Son so that the world through Him might be saved.

---

[64] John Piper (Referring to 1 John 2:2), *TULIP: What We Believe about the Five Points of Calvinism* (Minneapolis, Minn.: Desiring God Ministries, 1997), www.desiringgod.org.

"How is it more for the glory of God to save man irresistibly, than to save him as a free agent, by such grace as he may either concur or resist?"

-John Wesley

7

GRACE

God's grace is saving, liberating, empowering, and transforming. The gospel is the good news of the grace of God [Acts 20:24]. Grace has freed men from works salvation, legalism, condemnation and shame. Grace has brought us into a relationship with Christ free from duty and full of delight.

The revelation of the gospel of grace has caught fire in the twenty-first century. Turn on the TV or visit the local Christian bookstore, and you will find that the chief message of the Church is that of God's extravagant grace. However, along with the new "Grace Reformation" has come a counterfeit message of grace. Multitudes of sincere but immature believers have bought into an unbiblical hyper-grace expression of Christianity that has nothing to do with obedience to Jesus.

They are fulfilling the prophetic words of Jude that warn of a great-grace-perversion that will find its ultimate fulfillment at the end of the age.

> Jude 1:3,4 NIV "*Contend for the faith* that was once for all entrusted to God's holy people. For certain individuals... have secretly slipped in among you. They are ungodly people, who *pervert the grace of our God into a license for immorality* and *deny Jesus Christ* our only Lord."

Church leaders throughout the earth are dangerously misrepresenting the glory of God's grace for something cheap and easy.

Grace is being distorted and misused which has given birth to spiritual lukewarmness, sanctified sin, and sexual immorality among God's people. How often has someone preached a message on sin, holiness, or obedience, only to be reminded after the sermon to be careful lest they mix grace with law, works with salvation, legalism with obedience. From where are the people getting this? They have not learned it from the Bible.

The Apostle Paul, undoubtedly the premier grace preacher of the New Testament, continually balanced God's extravagant grace with radical obedience to His holy standards. Grace and obedience go hand in hand and never is one to be exalted at the expense of the other.

> "You don't have to repent! You are *already forgiven.*"

> "You don't have to obey or keep God's commands! Jesus obeyed fully for you."

> "You don't have to be conscious of sin! *God doesn't see your sin*; He only sees Jesus."

> "You don't have to focus on living righteously! You are the righteousness of God in Christ."

> "You don't have to strive to enter the kingdom! *Grace is effortless* and easy."

All of these grace phrases, noticeably half-true, I have heard from the lips of some of the most popular grace preachers on the planet. This is troubling. Grace is being distorted before our eyes, and with the help of mass media, it has instantly been transported to the ends of the earth. More than any other time in history we have to take Jude's prophetic warning to heart. We must contend for the faith!

In a similar manner to Jude, the Apostle Peter warns us that false teachers will emerge in the last days who lead many to hell through lies and deception. They will subtly bring in destructive heresies about God, His Word, and His holy standards. They will distort grace to unbiblical proportions and in doing so deny the very One who bought them.

> 2 Peter 2:1,2 "There will be false teachers among you, who will secretly bring in *destructive heresies*, even *denying the Lord* who bought them, and bring on themselves swift destruction. And *many will follow their destructive ways*, because of whom the way of truth will be blasphemed."

These warnings are not in Scripture for our entertainment. Real people will go to hell for a very long time because we have not guarded the gospel of grace with fiery zeal. Grace is not merely a subject to debate or argue over. Souls are in the balance. Lives are at stake. The eternal destiny of believers and unbelievers hinge upon what we honestly believe about God's extravagant grace.

THE TRUTH ABOUT SOVEREIGN GRACE

The distorting of grace is not a current phenomenon. For centuries, Biblical grace has been misrepresented and redefined by pastors and theologians alike. It should be no surprise that deceptions about grace extend far beyond compromised teaching that degrades holiness and promotes sanctified sin. Salvation itself has come under fire from those who minimize grace (promoting legalism and works-salvation) and those who exaggerate grace (promoting compromise and lukewarmness).

One such dangerous and unbiblical view of saving grace comes from Calvinism's Five Points called *Irresistible Grace* or *Sovereign Grace*. Some Calvinists prefer to use the term *effectual calling* or *effectual grace* because it sounds less forceful though they mean virtually the same thing.

Anyone familiar with Calvinism will recognize that the Five Points fit perfectly together both in content and order. So far we have found that Calvinism asserts that mankind is entirely unable to repent and believe (Total Depravity) and that God has sovereignly chosen to unconditionally select certain people for salvation (Unconditional Election); because of this the work of Christ is only efficient for and offered to them and not others (Limited Atonement).

The next letter in TULIP is "I" labeled after John Calvin's doctrine of *Irresistible Grace*. Irresistible Grace says that if God sovereignly and unconditionally elects whom He desires to save, *He, therefore, makes their salvation sure by irresistibly drawing them* to Himself. Someone who is elect from the foundation of the world cannot resist His will, reject His salvation, or fall away. They will be saved regardless, simply because God has already chosen them.

It only follows that if God chose someone for salvation, He will also keep them saved until the end (Perseverance of the Saints). It does not take a prophet to see that Calvinism's Five Points come together as a whole. To take out one petal of TULIP will wilt the entire flower and upend the whole system. Irresistible Grace is the logical outcome of Total Depravity, Unconditional Election, and Limited Atonement; thereby leading to final Perseverance.

The Pocket Dictionary of the Reformed Tradition affirms this connection by defining Irresistible Grace as,

> "The sovereign grace of God in regeneration *arising from election* and *leading toward final perseverance*."[65]

Calvinists and non-Calvinists affirm that mankind is radically depraved and in need of God's grace to be saved. However, Calvinism again takes these doctrines to extremes. In assuming that our depravity equates to "Total Inability," it concludes that it is impossible for someone to yield to God or put any faith in Him. Therefore, God must first regenerate and change the sinner's hard heart with grace that is overpowering and irresistible.

If someone does not repent, it is because God has not chosen them for salvation and has withheld it from them. Indeed, they cannot repent

---

[65] Kapic & Vander Lugt. *Pocket Dictionary of the Reformed Tradition* (Downers Grove, IL: InterVarsity Press, 2013), p. 64-65.

because God never ordained it. They are only recipients of common grace (general grace to all people that can be resisted) and are excluded from experiencing saving grace (effectual grace that saves the elect that cannot be resisted).

If perhaps someone does turn to Him in repentance they are doing precisely what God caused them to do in the first place by sovereignly and single-handedly bringing forth their salvation. They are elect without condition and for that reason are drawn without hindrance. God saves them despite them. He does not wait for sinners to repent and believe but moves upon their heart and causes them to be born again with His sovereign, irresistible, overwhelming grace.

According to Calvinism, *unbelievers are making no voluntary choice in their salvation*. All sinners, regardless of what they may believe at the altar, do not choose God with their libertarian free will. Calvinism says that God alone has chosen them, drawn them, and saved them by overcoming their hardness and changing their wills so that they would desire Him, repent and believe in the gospel.

The theological term for sovereign, irresistible grace is called *monergism*. Monergism is the belief that salvation is entirely the work of God from beginning to end. The Holy Spirit acts independently of the human will in redemption and regeneration. The opposite, Arminian view is called *synergism*, which says that salvation is the work of God in partnership with man. Synergism affirms that the human will, with the help of God's grace, cooperates with the Holy Spirit in the process of salvation.

On the one hand, Calvinists do not embrace the Arminian view of synergism because it makes humanity's free will choice "the decisive factor in salvation," which according to many Calvinists is another form of man-centered, works-salvation in which sinful men can boast.

On the other, Arminians reject the Calvinist view of monergism because it requires God to withhold salvation from the very people He loves and supposedly desires to be saved. This makes God the divine author and ultimate cause of the eternal suffering and torment of untold billions. For some unknown reason, God could save them and wants to save them, but refuses to do so for the more significant, *secret* purpose of being glorified before all men [1 Timothy 2:3,4; 2 Peter 3:9].

Calvinists often seek to get around this dilemma by asserting that God has two wills. One is a general or revealed will - that God loves all people and does desire them to be saved, though He refuses to offer them what He truly desires. The other is referred to by Calvinists as God's specific or secret will - that God loves the elect with an exclusive love and therefore only offers salvation to them. Somehow God is saddened and grieved that multitudes of sinners end up in hell though He created them for this purpose and willed it from eternity, yet He rejoices because the greater purpose of His glory is put on display by making His power known in damning them.

Roger Olsen sums this enigma up well in saying,

> "While non-Calvinists are willing to admit that high Calvinism is God-centered, they have good reason to wonder how exactly to distinguish between the God it centers itself on and Satan- except that *Satan wants all people damned to hell and God wants only a certain number damned to hell.* That may sound harsh, but it is the reason most Christians are not Calvinists."[66]

Precisely the same God that is behind Calvin's Unconditional Election and Limited Atonement is behind Sovereign Grace as well. God wants to promote His glory more than He wants men to be saved. Therefore, we are left inclined to think that the God of Calvinism doesn't want everyone to be saved, which is why He never offered salvation to them or make atonement for their sins at the cross.

When we think of Calvinism's Sovereign Grace, we have to look beyond the debate about the means of grace by which God chooses to save people and consider the type of God it promotes. Yes, He loves to flex His muscles and show His sovereignty, but is He the same God of Scripture who loves the world, wills that none perish, and shows no partiality?

---

[66] Roger E. Olsen. *Against Calvinism* (Grand Rapids: Zondervan, 2011), p. 159.

FORCED TO BE WILLING?

Like the rest of the Five Points, confusion abounds everywhere, especially in the logic behind Irresistible Grace and free will. Calvinism's affirmation of man's Total Depravity demands that God first change the heart of the unsaved through regeneration so that his once stubborn and unresponsive free will now become freely willing. The sinner who in one moment hated God, delighted in sin, and never desired to repent or believe, has now been changed through instantaneous Irresistible Grace. God forces them to do what they, only moments ago, never wanted in the first place.

Calvinists emphatically resist such language as being forced yet over and again it is implied in their theology of grace. A sinner would never and could never choose to put faith in Christ, and therefore God must necessarily cause them to believe in Him *against their wills*. As John Piper writes,

> "The doctrine of irresistible grace does not mean that every influence of the Holy Spirit cannot be resisted. It means that *the Holy Spirit can overcome all resistance* and make his influence irresistible... God is sovereign and can overcome all resistance when He wills... It should be obvious from this that *irresistible grace never implies that God forces us to believe against our will*. That would even be a contradiction in terms."[67]

In his first statement, Piper affirms that Calvinism's Irresistible Grace does not mean that the Holy Spirit cannot be resisted but that He can overcome all resistance by forcing our unwilling heart to will and desire Him. He then contradicts himself in saying, "Irresistible Grace never implies that God forces us to believe against our will."[68] One can only wonder how the Irresistible Grace of God can effectually work on

---
[67] John Piper, *TULIP: What We Believe about the Five Points of Calvinism* (Minneapolis, Minn.: Desiring God Ministries, 1997), www.desiringgod.org.
[68] Ibid.

an utterly sinful, unwilling person without influencing him to believe against his will.

Piper and many other Calvinists sound like a clanging brass on this issue. Somehow saving, Sovereign Grace irresistibly changes the unbelievers will without violating their free will. In a sermon entitled "Skeptical Grumbling and the Sovereign Grace of God," Piper said,

> "Those whom the Father draws, come to Me. And when we come, I'll say it again, and I'll say it over and over, *we come voluntarily*, with zero coercion. *We come freely*, with zero constraint."[69]

Likewise, Charles Spurgeon claimed,

> "A man is *not saved against his will*, but *he is made willing* by the operation of the Holy Ghost."[70]

The Arminian response to such doubletalk is that the very nature of "coming voluntarily" to Christ, as John Piper puts it, is because the sinner willingly made a choice to do so in response to His drawing grace. If Calvinism is true and Irresistible Grace made us willing when we were wholly and adamantly unwilling, salvation is no longer voluntary, but involuntary. Our salvation is ultimately forced and coerced without any real involvement or participation on our part. Calvinism's insistence of unwilling sinners being changed by God so that they willingly come to Christ is not only not in Scripture, but it is a complete contradiction of basic logic.

THE GAPS IN IRRESISTIBLE GRACE

What is worse than the un-common sense behind Irresistible Grace are

---

[69] John Piper, Sermon: *Skeptical Grumbling and Sovereign Grace*. 11/29/2009 www.desiringgod.org/sermons
[70] Charles H. Spurgeon. Sermons, Vol. 10, p. 309

the numerous Biblical passages that completely contradict it.[71] In Matthew 23 Jesus rebuked the Scribes and Pharisees for "shutting up the kingdom of heaven against men" and "not allowing" in those who desire to enter. If Jesus were a Calvinist, He would never have made such a statement, for man, according to Calvinism, cannot hinder another from entering the kingdom, nor get in the way of God's redemptive purposes of salvation.

> Matthew 23:13 "But woe to you, scribes and Pharisees, hypocrites! For *you shut up the kingdom of heaven against men*; for you neither go in yourselves, *nor do you allow those who are entering to go in*."

Likewise, in Luke 13 Jesus laments over Jerusalem for her hardness of heart and unwillingness to be gathered together under His wings. Why would Jesus be grieved at the Jewish people's rejection of Him if God ordained that they never turn to Him in the first place? Why would He be upset at something that ultimately glorifies Him? If Jesus were convinced of Calvinism, He would have never mourned over Jerusalem, having concluded that their unwillingness was proof that they were never meant to be recipients of Irresistible Grace.

> Luke 13:34 "O Jerusalem, Jerusalem, the one who kills the prophets and stones those who are sent to her! *How often I wanted to gather your children together, as a hen gathers her brood under her wings, but you were not willing*!"

Roger Olsen's analogy proves the absurdity of this claim saying, "Suppose a father has a love potion that would cause all of his children to love him and never rebel against him. *He gives it to some of his children but not others and then weeps because some of his children reject him and don't love him.* Who would take him seriously? Or, if they took him seriously, who

---

[71] Proverbs 1:22-26; Hosea 11:1-9; Psalm 78:10, 81:11-13; Acts 7:2-53; Luke 7:30, 18:18-30; Matthew 13:1-23, 21:28-32, 21:33-44; Acts 26:14 - [References taken from *"Whosoever Will," A Biblical and Theological Critique of Five-Point Calvinism*, by Steve Lemke and David Allen. P. 109-162.]

wouldn't think him insincere or a bit mad?"[72]

Later in Luke 14, Jesus spoke the Parable of the Great Supper as a picture of many who were invited to fellowship with Him in His kingdom yet rejected the invitation for earthly things. The Master was angry at those who declined and commanded His servants to compel more to come in that His house would be full [14:15-24]. If Irresistible Grace were real, the Master Himself would be a deceived lunatic having become enraged at those whom He invited to feast with Him but refused, though He foreordained that they never come.

Another such example is Matthew 19. Here Jesus taught of the dangers of wealth and how "it is easier for a camel to go through the eye of a needle than for a rich man to enter the kingdom." Jesus is stating that riches, as opposed to poverty, can make it harder to be saved. However, according to Calvinism's Irresistible Grace, all men - whether rich, poor or middle-class, cannot resist or be hindered from salvation if God wills it.

> Matthew 19:23,24 "Then Jesus said to His disciples, 'Assuredly, I say to you that *it is hard for a rich man* to enter the kingdom of heaven… Again I say, *it is easier* for a camel to go through the eye of a needle than for a rich man to enter the kingdom of God.'"

Lastly, in Revelation 3 Jesus confronts the Church of Laodicea and rebukes them for spiritual lukewarmness [3:14-22]. In love, He chastens and calls them to repent. Jesus is pictured standing at the door of the Church, knocking, and waiting for each to let Him in for true fellowship. He is not forcing them into a relationship but is calling, seeking, knocking. If Jesus believed Irresistible Grace this portrait of salvation would be bizarre, for God, according to Calvinism, does not patiently wait for our response to open the door, but always effectually moves in when He so chooses.

> Revelation 3:20 "Behold, *I stand at the door and knock*. If *anyone*

---

[72] Roger E. Olsen, *Against Calvinism* (Grand Rapids: Zondervan, 2011), p. 164.

hears My voice and opens the door, I will come in to him and dine with him, and he with Me."

THE MYSTERY OF JOHN 6

One of the prominent proof-texts for Calvinism's view of grace and election is John Chapter 6. To Calvinists, this passage, as well as Romans 9, infallibly proves that we are saved if and when God wills it. Man ultimately has no say or part in his salvation but is efficiently drawn to Jesus without restraint. After all, Jesus said,

> John 6:37 "All that the Father gives Me will *come to Me*, and the one who *comes to Me* I will by no means cast out."

> John 6:44 "No one *can come to Me* unless the Father who sent Me *draws* him; and I will raise him up at the last day."

> John 6:64,65 "'But there are some of you who do not believe.' For *Jesus knew from the beginning who they were who did not believe*, and who would betray Him. And He said, 'Therefore I have said to you that no one can *come to Me* unless it has been granted to him by My Father.'"

In each of these passages, you will notice one phrase from Jesus that is repeated over and again. It is the phrase *"come to Me."* But the question at hand is how exactly does a sinner come to Jesus? By coercion and Irresistible Grace? By forcing an unwilling heart to be made willing? By showing partiality to certain sinners, while passing over those who are just as undeserving? By only drawing a few who are specially elect and damning billions who never had a choice to be saved to the praise of the glory of His grace?

Calvinists often wrongly translate the Greek word "draws" in John 6:44 as "compels" [Sproul], "impels" [Pink] or "drags" [Boettner] as clear evidence for Irresistible Grace that is always efficacious in saving the elect. However, the same word is used in John 12:32 speaking of God "drawing all men to Himself" through the cross. A Calvinist, who did not have a double standard, would, therefore, be forced to embrace universalism and concede that John 12:32 affirms that God is compelling or irresistibly drawing *all men* to Himself.

Arminians, however, do not argue the fact that the Father draws and grants unbelievers to come to Jesus, and that because of our sin no one will approach Him apart from God first drawing man. These are sure in light of the entirety of Scripture. God calls and draws all men, yet in His foreknowledge knows from the beginning who will not believe [John 6:64].

What is powerful about John 6 is that it stands in the context of the entire Gospel of John, which from beginning to end reveals how men "come to Jesus." God did not make this complicated. The Father simply grants sinners to come to the Son by believing and trusting in Him. This theme is the whole purpose of John's Gospel [John 1:7,12; 3:15, 16, 18, 36; 5:24; 6:35, 40, 47; 7:38; 8:24; 11:25, 26; 12:44, 46; 14:2; 20:31].

> John 1:7 "[John bore witness to the light] that *all* through Him *might believe*."
>
> John 1:12 "*As many as received Him*, to them He gave the right to become children of God, to *those who believe* in His name."
>
> John 3:15 "*Whoever believes* in Him should not perish but have eternal life."
>
> John 6:40 "*Everyone who sees the Son and believes in Him* may have everlasting life; and I will raise him up at the last day."
>
> John 7:37, 38 "*If anyone* thirsts, let him come to Me and drink. *He who believes* in Me, as the Scripture has said, out of his heart will flow rivers of living water."

John 12:36 "*Believe* in the light, *that you may become* sons of light."

John 20:31 "These are written that you may *believe* that Jesus is the Christ, the Son of God, and that *believing you may have life* in His name."

Never does John tell us that those the Father gives to Jesus are a particular group of elect people who are sovereignly regenerated before they believe. Instead, Scripture makes plain that all whom the Father gives to the Son are the ones who trust in His salvation and are saved.

Noticeably, before John 6, Jesus rebuked men who resisted Him because they were *"not willing to come"* that they may have life [John 5:40]. Here Jesus highlights their rejection of Him based upon their free will choice. Again if Calvinism were correct, it would be foolishness for Jesus to make such a statement simply because when God chooses to give someone life, He automatically changes their will thereby causing them to come to Him.

PREVENIENT GRACE

The Arminian view of grace is not an arbitrary, impartial grace bestowed upon some and not others. Instead, saving grace is an undeserved, unmerited favor offered to all people [Titus 2:11]. It is an expression of God's kindness towards us though we are undeserving and unworthy of salvation.

The Bible portrays God's grace as both powerful and prevenient; however, it is never pictured as something that is forced upon us. The saving grace of God enables us to respond to His supernatural drawing which produces a heart of repentance and faith within us. God is and forever will be the sovereign initiator and source of salvation, yet man has a vital part to play in God's saving purposes. A.W. Tozer describes this Divine / human partnership of saving grace saying,

> "Christian theology teaches the doctrine of *prevenient grace*, which briefly stated means this, that before a man can seek God, God must first have sought the man... We pursue God because, and only because, He has first put an urge within us that spurs us to the pursuit. "No man can come to me," said our Lord, "except the Father which hath sent me draw him," and it is by this very prevenient drawing that God takes from us every vestige of credit for the act of coming. *The impulse to pursue God originates with God, but the outworking of that impulse is our following hard after Him*; and all the time we are pursuing Him we are already in His hand: "Thy right hand upholdeth me."[73]

Through grace, God makes way for humanity to come to Him yet He does so without manipulating them to receive Him against their will. Grace always comes from God freely and fully as an unearned favor. It is a free gift that must be received by faith [Ephesians 2:8].

The nature of grace itself proves that it can be refused, resisted or rejected. Men can fall short of God's grace [Hebrews 12:15], fall from grace [Galatians 5:4], and receive the grace of God in vain [2 Corinthians 6:1]. Calvinism again seeks a way around these verses by placing them in the category of "general grace" to all people, not saving grace for the elect.

The heart of the matter is that God does not force man into fellowship simply because love is never coerced. God is after relationship, not robots. As Roger Olsen writes, "Common sense alone dictates that a truly *personal relationship always involves free will*; insofar as one party controls the other such that the other has no real choice whether to be in the relationship or not, is *not a real relationship*."[74]

God desires that that we delight in Him forever, not because we *have to* but because we *want to*. God's people for all time, stand in voluntary love beneath the shadow of a sovereign God.

---

[73] A.W. Tozer. *The Pursuit of God* (Camp Hill PA: Christian Publications, 1993), p. 11.
[74] Roger E. Olsen, *Against Calvinism* (Grand Rapids: Zondervan, 2011), p. 168.

"When God saves you, He doesn't do it because you gave Him permission. He did it because He's God."

-Matt Chandler

8

FAITH

Growing up in a Charismatic, Faith Church in the 80's and 90's was interesting, to say the least. Prophecy, faith, healing, prosperity, Jimmy Swaggart, PTL, and Jim Bakker were all hot topics that swept through the Church like a warm breeze on a humid day. You didn't know whether you preferred the wind or wished it would go away because it only made you all the more sweaty and uncomfortable.

Deep down I knew the Charismatic movement had a lot of issues, but I also had a sense that Jesus was pleased with our weak and often immature hunger. We would rather have all of God than none of Him, which in time led to excesses and errors. Because this movement was somewhat new, leaders were forced to learn many things the hard way through trial and error, the leading of the Spirit, and Biblical guidelines outlined in God's Word.

As with anything in life, with the good came the bad. As someone once said, "No one ever seeks to counterfeit of a penny." Satan only tries to distort and corrupt that which is highly valuable and dangerous to Him. If there were false prophets, true prophetic voices were hiding in a cave somewhere. False miracles and healings proved Jesus still does them today. The lie of name-it-and-claim-it only added more evidence to the fact that our faith, and our words, matter to God and influence what happens on the earth.

Rather than throw out the baby with the bath water, there were many faith lessons to be learned if we were humble enough to receive them. Faith in God is a powerful conduit between weak men and an omnipotent God. Though God is sovereign and does what He pleases, He also requires something from us. His saving, redemptive activity in the earth is intimately connected to the active faith, obedience, and partnership of man. This co-labor between God and man is the essence of faith. We certainly cannot do God's part, and He will not do ours.

SALVATION BY FAITH

At the very beginning of our journey into faith in Christ, we discover that we are saved by grace *through faith* – not works! No amount of charitable deeds or self-righteous efforts can get us into the kingdom. All of our giving, serving and sacrificing for God and man will never earn us a ticket to heaven. Our depravity is far too great, and God's holiness is far too glorious.

Like an ant setting out to conquer Mt. Everest, the unbeliever, who is "good enough" to somehow get into the kingdom will realize that the task is utterly impossible. He cannot get there no matter how much he tries. His self-effort apart from faith in Christ is the ultimate statement of sin and pride. He is putting faith in himself and his strivings, not in the saving work of Jesus Christ.

In the Bible, salvation is by grace alone, through faith alone, in Christ alone, for God's glory alone! The truth of Luther's reformation stands firm as the bedrock of Christian belief. The only way that one is declared righteous before God and justified in His sight is through faith [Galatians 2:16]. As Arminius states,

> "Faith, and faith only, (though there is no faith alone without works,) is imputed for righteousness. *By this alone we are justified before God*, absolved of our sins, and are accounted, pronounced and declared righteous by God, who delivers His judgment from the throne of grace."[75]

---

[75] Jacobus Arminius. *The Works of James Arminius* (University of VA General Library, 1819), p. 473.

The essence of God's grace is revealed in the fact that we are saved through faith. Paul could call it *"the gospel of the grace of God"* because the good news is that faith alone, confirmed by works, is what brings us into the redemptive benefits of salvation [Acts 20:24]. Self-righteous works in themselves have never brought a man closer to God. Not in the Old Testament. Not in the New Testament. Not now. Not ever. We are saved by grace through faith unto good works.

> Ephesians 2:8,9 *"By grace* you have been *saved through faith*, and that not of yourselves; it is the gift of God, *not of works*, lest anyone should boast. For we are His workmanship, created in Christ Jesus *for good works*, which God prepared beforehand that we should walk in them."

Faith is where all of Christianity begins and ends. It is the conduit through which sinful men and women have access to a holy God. There is no salvation without it. Apart from active believing and trusting in Jesus Christ for salvation from our sins, we are all consigned to an eternity in the lake of fire. True faith is the key that opens the door of the kingdom, brings us through it, and keeps us there forever [Romans 10:9; James 2:23].

> Acts 16:30 "'What must I do to be saved?' '...*Believe on the Lord Jesus Christ, and you will be saved*, you and your household.'"

THE ACTION OF FAITH

God is a God of faith. In His wisdom, He has established faith as the means by which someone experiences His manifold blessings. All of the benefits and provisions of the Kingdom of God including salvation, healing, miracles, and answered prayer are appropriated by faith [Galatians 3:5]. The virtue of faith not only pleases God, but it moves His generous hand and makes the impossible possible [Hebrews 11:1,6; Mark 11:23,24].

> Mark 9:23 "*If* you can *believe*, all things are possible to him who *believes.*"

Biblical faith is not merely a belief, but an action; which is why James can say, "faith without *works* is dead" [James 2:14-21]. The act of faith is the believer's willful, voluntary response of trust and confidence in Christ that results in joyful obedience. Faith is the product of our voluntary submission to the Holy Spirit and surrender to God the Father's will. *It is never something God does for us!* Instead, it is something we do that positions us to receive the many benefits of God's redeeming grace.

Jesus understood the importance of faith and revealed its true nature in the Gospels. Faith was never irresistible because of grace, nor guaranteed because of unconditional election. People who had not yet been born again had the ability to put their trust in Jesus whether it be for salvation, provision, or healing; and God responded to their active faith with transforming demonstrations of His power.

> Mark 5:34 "He [Jesus] said to her, 'Daughter, *your faith* has made you well. Go in peace, and be healed of your affliction.'"

> Matthew 8:13 "Jesus said to the centurion, 'Go your way; and *as you have believed, so let it be done for you.*' And his servant was *healed that same hour.*"

> Matthew 9:20-22 "Daughter; *your faith has made you well.*" And the woman was made well from that hour."

The Book of Acts tells the same story. Faith is the connecting point of heaven and earth, God and man. Faith lays hold of eternity and pulls down every blessing of redemption. Faith positions weak and broken vessels to receive supernatural interventions of God's power [Acts 6:8]. Faith aligns man with God our Savior, our Healer, our Redeemer, our Deliverer, our All in All.

> Acts 3:16 "His name, *through faith* in His name, has made this man strong…"
>
> Acts 14:9,10 "Paul… *seeing that he had faith to be healed*, said with a loud voice, 'Stand up straight on your feet!' And he leaped and walked."

Just as with salvation, man does not work up divine healing or create it merely because they want it. Faith alone, with the help of the Holy Spirit, is the fulcrum that affects His sovereign, saving, healing hand. James tells us it is the prayer *offered in faith* that saves the sick, but always it is the Lord who will raise him up [James 5:15].

If simple, child-like faith moves the heart and hand of God, so unbelief within our heart displeases Him and hinders the release of His supernatural power. The Son of God Himself could not do many mighty works in His hometown for this very reason. The lack of faith was apparently not on Jesus' part but theirs. Though God is all powerful, the act of unbelief kept the kingdom of God from coming in power.

> Matthew 13:58 "Now He did *not do* many mighty works there because of their *unbelief*."
>
> Mark 6:5,6 "Now He could do no mighty work there, except that *He laid His hands on a few sick people and healed them*. And He marveled because of their *unbelief*."

Whether regenerate or unregenerate, the Bible shows us that every human being is created with the capacity to believe in Christ. It only takes a small mustard seed so that the power of the age to come to break forth on the earth. This principle is also true of faith's relationship to salvation. In Luke 7 Jesus displayed the greatest miracle of all, that of salvation, to a sinful woman. By turning from her sin and actively believing in Christ, God accounted her faith to her for salvation.

> Luke 7:50 "He said to the woman, '*Your faith* has *saved you*. Go in peace.'"

Whose faith was it that saved her? Was it *God's faith* irresistibly and unconditionally imparted by grace? No! *Her faith* is what saved her. Fourteen times in the Gospels Jesus says the phrase *"your faith"* to prove that faith is an action that *man does* out of reckless trust in the goodness of God. Never once does Jesus commend believers for being passive recipients of this magical gift of God's faith.

Surprisingly, Reformed Calvinism teaches that faith is not only something that *God does* as an act of His sovereign will but that it is impossible for an unbeliever to exercise any faith unless they are first born again. To the Calvinist, this view of faith preserves the glory of God, making salvation "entirely a work of God" from beginning to end.

To get around such blatant verses that prove depraved people can believe, as in the case of the woman in Luke 7, Calvinists claim that a secret and unknown work of regeneration happens before faith comes into existence. Somewhere, somehow, in some way unknown to the Calvinist, God decided to change the sinner's unwilling heart to want Him so that they have the capacity to believe.

> "*Regeneration comes before saving faith*... This secret, hidden work of God in our spirits does in fact come *before we respond to God in saving faith*."[76]

In the quote above Wayne Grudem is affirming the Calvinist position that we are sovereignly born again before we put faith in Jesus for salvation. In this view faith is not so much a voluntary *action* that we do, but an involuntary *response* of faith in His call. Faith is ultimately an act that God does as He irresistibly imparts it to the sinner based upon sovereign grace. Calvinism's doctrine of faith is always the outworking of Irresistible Grace.

---

[76] Wayne Grudem, Systematic Theology (Grand Rapids: Zondervan, 1994, 2002), p. 702

To add insult to injury Grudem goes on to insist that this is not how we should apply the gospel (i.e., in preaching to others) but instead we must call all men to believe. This double talk makes one wonder why such a secret work of regeneration that Calvinists seem to know so much about should be kept top secret until the unregenerate is converted through an Arminian presentation of the gospel. According to Grudem, we are to believe in Calvinism's view of saving faith, but not necessarily apply it when preaching salvation to sinners.

> "*By way of application*, we should realize that the explanation of the gospel message in Scripture *does not* take the form of a command, "Be born again and you will be saved," but rather, "Believe in Jesus Christ and you will be saved." *This is the consistent pattern of the preaching of the gospel...*"[77]

Calvinist theology ultimately believes that our depravity demands God to save sinful people apart from our initial, willing participation of faith. In other words, God saved and will continue to save men because they are elect, not because they repent and believe. God does not save us because we did something and put faith in Jesus, but we believed because God did something in us by causing us to believe.

> "*We do not believe in order to be born again*; we are born again in order that we may believe."[78]

> "*A man is not regenerated because he first believed* in Christ, but he believes in Christ because he has been regenerated."[79]

As stated earlier, this Calvinist belief called "monergism" says that when God sets Himself to save the elect, He saves! He doesn't need our help or our cooperation. Faith is something God does in our hearts after we have been born again by His Spirit. The story goes that if perhaps you

---

[77] Ibid.
[78] R.C. Sproul, *Chosen By God* (Wheaton: Tyndale House, 1986), p. 73.
[79] Arthur W. Pink, *The Holy Spirit* (Grand Rapids: Baker Book House, 1978), p. 55.

are one of the elect ones who has been fortunate enough to win the lottery of heaven and be predestined to glory; God will regenerate you, impart faith, and grant repentance in His own time and way!

This sovereign, secret choice of God has nothing to do with any action of man, or any foreseen faith or virtue in man, but based on His Unconditional Election! Your salvation has nothing to do with whether you believe or not (it is impossible if you are not of the elect), but whether God had chosen you to believe in the first place.

Many Calvinists affirm that one must believe the gospel and repent to be converted, but this act of faith itself is a gift of God. After all, Paul says that *"by grace you have been saved through faith ...it is a gift of God"* [Ephesians 2:8]. However, in this context, faith is not the "gift of God" Paul is speaking of, but the gift of salvation. God grants men to believe in Him (just as He gives men repentance) through His enabling grace, but He never forces it upon them through Irresistible Grace, because it does not exist [Philippians 1:29, 2 Timothy 2:25].

RECEIVING SALVATION BY FAITH

The Bible says that God saves those who believe [Acts 16:30,31; Mark 16:16; Luke 8:12; John 12:36, 20:31; 1 Corinthians 1:21, Romans 1:16, 10:9]. Faith, our initial and ongoing trust in Jesus, is necessary and vital to salvation from beginning to end. Nowhere does Scripture say that God covertly regenerates people whom He has chosen before the foundations of the world apart from their active response of faith in His call!

Thomas Oden rightly proclaims,

> "The benefits of Christ's atoning work are applied by the Spirit and *appropriated by the believer through faith*... Faith is the only condition required for a reconciled relationship to the Giver of Life. Faith is the *primary condition* for the *reception* of every subsequent stage of God's saving activity."[80]

---

[80] Thomas C. Oden, *Classic Christianity- A Systematic Theology* (New York, NY: HarperCollins, 1992), p. 596,599.

Saving faith is personal trust in a living Savior followed by a lifetime of willful obedience. It is always our voluntary, personal response to God's grace. Therefore it is freely given by God and freely received by man. Never is it coerced or compelled, as if God, through an unknown act of regeneration, flips a switch within the human will and makes one believe through grace that is irresistible.

When it comes to salvation, God will not do our part, and we cannot do His! Grace is always *God's part* in salvation; however, faith (or responding to His grace) is *ours*. The Apostle Paul confirmed this when he said that we have "*access by faith into this grace*" in which we stand [Romans 5:1,2]. Faith always accesses the grace of God for salvation but never does God's effectual grace automatically produce saving faith.

We are not saved by our faith, but solely because of His grace. However, we appropriate God's grace for salvation by putting our faith in the Lord Jesus. As theologian I. Howard Marshall writes, "Faith, which is the biblical word for *the human response to God's grace*, is simply the holding out of our hands to receive the divine gift. There is nothing to do except receive what God graciously offers us... *A person who comes to God must believe that he exists* and rewards those who seek him [Hebrews 11:6]."[81]

The Bible tells us that a believer's faith toward God is not a one-time act of grace that God does in and of Himself, but it is a *continuous lifestyle* of trusting and obeying Jesus. Faith is what the just *live by* and *walk in*, not something that strictly happens once, the moment that we are regenerated by the Holy Spirit [Habakkuk 2:4; Galatians 3:12].

Romans 1:17 "The just shall *live by faith*."

2 Corinthians 5:7 "We *walk by faith*, not by sight."

Hebrews 10:38 "Now the just shall *live by faith*."

---

[81] I Howard Marshall. *A New Testament Theology*, The Life of the Christian. www.biblicaltraining.org.

Such verses prove this without dispute. Faith must be *exercised continually* if it is true saving faith. As Bible teacher David Pawson writes, "Faith is not a single step, but many, many steps, a walk, indeed, *a journey of a lifetime*. It is not the faith we start with but *the faith we finish with* that lands us safe in glory."[82] In other words, as we work out and walk out salvation we go from faith to faith and from glory to glory by the Spirit of the Lord [Philippians 2:12; 2 Corinthians 3:18].

The Greek word *faith* in Scripture (*pistis*) is the same word used for *faithfulness*. Therefore to be full of faith means *to be faithful* in the continuous present tense [Revelation 17:14]. In the same way, it is impossible to claim to have faith and yet live unfaithfully. Faith displayed through obedience is a constant lifestyle that God requires every single believer to engage in their entire life.

> Revelation 2:10 "Be *faithful* [full of faith] *until death* [your whole life, until you die], and I will give you the crown of life."

Being saved and sustained by faith until death contradicts the view of Unconditional Eternal Security that says a believer will still be saved even when he "departs from faith" during his life.[83] Nowhere in Scripture do we find that a one-time act of faith is enough to sustain our eternal salvation. We must continue in a life of faith and obedience to Christ if we are to stand blameless before Him in that Day.

> Colossians 1:22,23 "In the body of His flesh through death, to present you holy, and blameless, and above reproach in His sight— *if indeed you continue in the faith*, grounded and steadfast, and are *not moved away* from the hope of the gospel…"

True, saving, continuous faith in Christ and His atonement is the only foundation of our assurance. God Himself promises that He will

---

[82] David Pawson, *Once Saved, Always Saved?* (London: Hodder, 1996), p. 21.
[83] See Chapter 9 on Perseverance. Most Reformed Calvinists would reject this notion and believe that if someone turned away from faith in Christ, they are not eternally secure, having never been saved in the first place.

present us holy, blameless, and above reproach in His sight *if we continue in faith* and are not moved away from the hope of the gospel. Paul's conditional clause (if) shows that he, through the inspiration of the Spirit, never took salvation for granted even among true believers!

> Acts 11:23 "[Barnabas] encouraged them all that with purpose of heart they should *continue with the Lord.*"

> Acts 13:43 "…Paul and Barnabas, who, speaking to them, persuaded them to *continue in the grace of God.*"

> Acts 14:22 "[Paul] strengthening the souls of the disciples, exhorting them to *continue in the faith*, and saying, 'We must through many tribulations enter the kingdom of God.'"

Because faith is not an irresistible gift given by Unconditional Election man has a significant and active role in His salvation. Indeed, God has grafted us into Israel's family tree, but *we must continue* in His goodness *through faith* lest we too miss out on the life that is in the Vine. As we will see plainly in the next chapter, faith in Jesus, manifest through obedience, is the only assurance of our salvation from beginning to end.

> Romans 11:22,23 "Consider the goodness and severity of God: on those who fell severity; but toward you, goodness, *if you continue* in His goodness. *Otherwise you also will be cut off.* And they [Israel] also, if they do not continue in unbelief, will be grafted in, for God is able to graft them in again."

Believers who depart from faith and cease to continue will also be cut off by God just as Israel was cut off due to unbelief [Romans 11:20]. We, with the assistance of grace, must hold fast our confidence by faith firm to the end.

> Hebrews 3:6,12,14 "Christ as a Son over His house, whose house we are *if we hold fast* the confidence and rejoicing of the hope *firm to the end*... Beware, *brethren*, lest there be in any of you an evil heart of unbelief in *departing from the living God*... For we have become partakers of Christ *if we hold* the beginning of our confidence *steadfast to the end*."

The mystery of how regeneration and grace work with faith is not too mysterious. The act of faith is nothing less than our voluntary response to God's grace by which we are born again. Yes, God enables and assists our believing. However, He does not make it inevitable or guarantee its eternal existence because Calvinism says so. Saving grace is available to all men [Titus 2:11], and all who believe the gospel will be saved [Romans 3:22; Acts 16:31; 1 Corinthians 1:21].

> Acts 15:11 "We *believe* that through the *grace* of the Lord Jesus Christ we shall be *saved*."

"I will be an infidel at one when I can believe that a saint of God can ever fall finally. If God hath loved me once, then He will love me forever."

-C.H. Spurgeon

9

PERSEVERANCE

The Christian trusts in a God who keeps His people from falling.[84] Call it what you want… Perseverance. Preservation. Security. Assurance. The Biblical conclusion remains the same. If you continue in Christ through faith, He will keep you in His grace [Colossians 1:22,23]. There is no fear of hell, eternal judgment, or falling away, when we stumble at times in various sins or make the slightest mistake. We can be sure that the power of God keeps us through faith firm until the end.

Jesus could not have made it any simpler.

> John 10:27-29 "My sheep hear My voice, and I know them, and *they follow Me*. And I give them eternal life, and they shall never perish; *neither shall anyone snatch them out of My hand*. My Father, who has given them to Me, is greater than all; and *no one is able to snatch them out of My Father's hand*."

In one sweeping statement, Jesus summed up the debate about perseverance. His sheep, both believing Jews, and Gentiles who have entered by Him and are saved, and who *follow Him* in the continuous present tense need not fear another stealing their eternal salvation [John 10:9, 16, 27]. They are safe in His arms. No one can snatch them out of the Father's hand. As the favorite hymn "In Christ Alone" goes,

---

[84] I Howard Marshall. *A New Testament Theology*, The Life of the Christian. www.biblicaltraining.org.

> "No power of hell, no scheme of man,
> Can ever pluck me from His hand;
> Till He returns or calls me home-
> Here in the power of Christ I'll stand."

The doctrine of Christ's commitment to keeping us strengthens our heart in God and fills us with confidence in His grace. God is powerful to uphold, protect and sustain us in His love until the end. God's power is much bigger than our weakness. When we discover that we cannot keep ourselves in salvation apart from His grace, we are liberated to surrender wholly to Him who is more than willing to perfect the work that He has started within us.

> Philippians 1:6 "Being confident of this very thing, that *He who has begun a good work in you will complete it* until the day of Christ."

Like Jesus, the Apostle Paul was utterly persuaded of this reality. He was convinced of it. He knew the heart of Him in whom he believed and was confident that He would keep the things he has committed to Him, including His eternal salvation, until that day [2 Timothy 1:12]. Paul knew that God would never let him down. He could trust Him with his life- his sinful past, his present salvation, and his eternal future, without reserve.

In every Church, Paul continually reminded faithful believers to rejoice with confidence in God's steadfast love. Just as no man could snatch them out of God's hand, neither could anyone separate them from God's love. Paul loved and lived this reality. It was the air that he breathed. No power, no principality, no present circumstance, no difficulty, and not even death itself can separate us from God's relentless love found in Christ.

> Romans 8:38,39 "Neither death nor life, nor angels nor principalities nor powers, nor things present nor things to come, nor height nor depth, nor any other created thing, shall be *able to separate us from the love of God* which is in Christ Jesus our Lord."

As complex as men have made the doctrine of Perseverance out to be it is very simple! We are *kept and preserved by His power through faith* until our salvation is wholly revealed when Christ returns in glory [1 Peter 1:5]. When that day comes, we will stand before Him with nothing to boast in but the cross, and the keeping, sustaining power of the Holy Spirit that worked powerfully within us all of our days.

CALVINISM'S OBSESSION WITH PERSEVERANCE

Before you jump on the eternal security bandwagon, we must consider the full council of God's Word. There is much more to say in Scripture about it than the positive perseverance verses just mentioned. We must be careful lest we present an unbalanced view of perseverance that promotes compromise and at the end of the day damns people to hell. This error is a grave and present danger within the Church today.

Charles Stanley, a famous TV evangelist and Southern Baptist Pastor writes,

> "Even if a believer for all practical purposes becomes an unbeliever, his salvation is not in jeopardy... *believers who lose or abandon their faith will retain their salvation...* You and I are not saved because we have enduring faith. We are saved because at a moment in time we expressed faith in our enduring Lord."[85]

I cannot think of a statement more dangerous and unbiblical than that. Not only is it not in Scripture, but it comforts compromising believers (who are saved and struggling with sin) and gives confidence to false converts (who have never been saved) that they are eternally secure because they prayed a magical prayer of faith one time in their life.

Christians everywhere have bought into this deception. We have taken sin lightly because leaders have not taught the passages of comfort *and* warning concerning the believer's perseverance. We have stopped at the glorious promises of salvation, having put them on our mugs and t-

---

[85] Charles Stanley. *Eternal Security: Can You Be Sure?* (Nashville: Oliver Nelson, 1990); pg. 1-5; 80.

shirts, but have not honestly grappled with the Biblical warnings of falling away that root us in the holy fear of the Lord.

For some reason, the doctrine of eternal security has become an obsession within the American Church, especially among Reformed Calvinists. I seriously wonder if the measure that we have clung to this doctrine proves the measure of our spiritual complacency and lukewarmness. Why is the assurance of salvation so important to us? Why do we fight for it more than we contend for the First Commandment [Matthew 22:37]? If we are living a life of radical repentance and faith while loving Jesus with all of our heart, we have no reason to worry! So why the big fuss?

For starters, Calvinism's obsession with perseverance is not because they love the doctrine itself more than they love Jesus. Rather they love Calvinism. And in Calvinist theology, the eternal security of the believer is the necessary outcome of the previous four points of TULIP.

If one holds to the belief that mankind's depravity is the equivalent of having no free will to choose God (Total Depravity) and that God has predestined some for salvation before time (Unconditional Election) having died for their sins only (Limited Atonement), and that God must irresistibly draw the elect to Himself by regenerating their heart before they believe (Irresistible Grace), one has necessarily to believe that a genuine Christian cannot fall away or forfeit their salvation (Perseverance of the Saints).

The Westminster Confession of Faith defines the Reformed view of perseverance saying,

> "They whom God hath accepted in His Beloved, effectually called and sanctified by His Spirit, can *neither totally nor finally fall away from the state of grace*; but shall certainly persevere therein to the end, and be eternally saved."[86]

Pastor Tom Ross, a Calvinist Baptist rightly adds,

---

[86] Westminster Confession of Faith, Chapter 17, sec. 1.

> "If they [Arminians] deny total depravity, unconditional election, particular redemption, and effectual calling, *they must of necessity also deny the saint's final perseverance*. All of the doctrines of grace form a harmonious whole. They stand or fall together. It is inconsistent to embrace one of the five points and not all."[87]

The Fifth Point of Calvinism is the "P" in TULIP called the "*Perseverance of the Saints.*" This descriptive title can be deceptive because it is not so much the perseverance of the saints, but rather the *preservation of the elect* that is in view. The Christian does not persevere as though he were in some way keeping watch over his salvation but is preserved by God strictly because of his election from the foundation of the earth.

Calvinism needs the doctrine of Perseverance to uphold all of the previous points. If TULIP stopped with the "I" and taught that one could fall away or commit apostasy from the faith, the entire system would be riddled with confusion and contradiction. Unconditional Election and Irresistible Grace require the doctrine of Perseverance to stand, which is why it is so vehemently defended and exalted to unbiblical proportions among Calvinists. Any hint of the possibility of someone falling away derails Calvinism as a whole.

THE FOUR POINTS OF PERSEVERANCE

Calvinists describe the Perseverance of the Saints in four primary ways:

First, *Calvinism teaches that God will always preserve the elect until the end based on their unconditional election, not conditional perseverance.* Predestination (as understood by Calvinists) implies that those who were chosen before the foundation of the earth cannot lose their salvation in any circumstances. Therefore, true believers are eternally secure.

Second, *Calvinism affirms that true regeneration and perseverance of the elect will always manifest itself in godly living after one's conversion.* God not only keeps the elect on the highway to heaven, but He also keeps them holy. They

---

[87] Tom Ross, *Abandoned Truth: The doctrines of Grace* [Xenia: Providence Baptist Church, 1991]; p. 91.

may stumble into sin, but they will not persist in sin. If they do, it is evidence that the believer was never saved or regenerated by God's power.

Third, *Calvinism asserts that if those who seem to be elect, but are not, fall away or turn away from the faith, they too were never saved in the first place.* To answer the numerous examples of genuine believers turning from God because of willful sin, hardness of heart, or unbelief, they must conclude that they were never of the elect. Though the sinner thought they were born again and regenerated by the Holy Spirit, they were false converts. They professed an empty faith and their falling away is proof that God's sovereign decree never elected them.

Fourth, *Calvinism concludes that if those who are elect seem to fall away or backslide, they will return to the faith before they die.* Like the Parable of the Prodigal Son, the rebellious child of God may go through seasons of backsliding and for a time leave the father's house, but God's Irresistible Grace will always effectually bring them back before they die [Luke 15:11-32]. Being elect, they do not have a choice in the matter. They will always return to the Father without fail.

These four principles, in a nutshell, are Calvinism's doctrine of Perseverance. The believer's eternal salvation is not due to the *perseverance of the saints* as much as it is the *preservation of God*. God irresistibly saves the men whom He has elected, and therefore He will keep them saved because they are elect. It is impossible for them to fall away!

John Piper affirms that perseverance is based on election in saying,

> "This is why we believe in eternal security--namely, the *eternal security of the elect.* the implication is that God will so work that *those whom he has chosen* for eternal salvation will be enabled by him to persevere in faith to the end and fulfill, by the power of the Holy Spirit, the requirements for obedience."[88]

---

[88] John Piper, *TULIP: What We Believe about the Five Points of Calvinism* (Minneapolis, Minn.: Desiring God Ministries, 1997), www.desiringgod.org.

In direct opposition to the Calvinist version of perseverance stands the Arminian. By disagreeing with Calvinism's extreme view of Unconditional Election, he necessarily disagrees with their view of perseverance. Men are not saved and kept saved because they were predestined to do so by God's eternal decree, but they are saved and kept saved through present faith in the Lord Jesus.

> 1 John 5:13 "These things I have written to you who believe… that you may *know* [i.e., Biblical assurance] *that you have eternal life*, and that you may *continue to believe* in the name of the Son of God."

The power of the Gospel unto our eternal salvation is only made effective *by believing* and *continuing to believe* in Jesus [Romans 1:16]. Never is the believer saved by faith and kept saved by performing good works. Though works can rightly prove if our salvation is genuine, they never are the guarantee of our eternal security [James 2:14-26; Galatians 2:16, 3:3, 5:4,5]. We are saved by faith, sustained by faith, and kept by faith alone.

> Galatians 5:5 "We through the Spirit eagerly wait for the hope of righteousness *by faith*."

Along with Calvinists, Arminians agree that multitudes of people in the Church today who profess to be believers are no more saved than the pagan down the road. The Church is filled with false converts and unregenerate counterfeit-Christians.

But unlike Calvinism, they are not false converts because they believed in Christ and yet were not among the exclusive group of elect people chosen before the world began. They are false converts because they never sincerely repented and believed in the way that Scripture commands. Their faith in Jesus was never real and authentic in the first place. It was fake, and therefore, their empty belief was in vain.

> 1 Corinthians 15:1,2 "I declare to you the gospel... in which you stand, by which also *you are saved*, if you hold fast that word which I preached... *unless you believed in vain.*"
>
> Luke 8:12 "Those by the wayside are the ones who hear; then the devil comes and takes away the word out of their hearts, lest they should *believe and be saved.*"

Having never been saved and regenerated by God, unbelievers - who claim to be believers, naturally cannot fall away. They are already fallen having never experienced true salvation. Their name may slip away from our Church membership log, but they cannot fall away from the faith. It is impossible for them to commit apostasy. One cannot turn back from the faith that they never truly had faith in.

It also goes to say that neither would someone who is unsaved need warned of falling away! They do not need to be exhorted to be careful "lest they drift away," if they are already fallen and drifting towards destruction [Hebrews 2:1]. This type of warning found throughout Scripture will always be pointless and to no avail. Someone who is non-elect need not be concerned about falling away for they have nothing to fall away from having never been appointed to salvation in the first place.

WARNINGS OF FALLING AWAY

So why does Scripture give so many warnings to believers of falling away? And is it possible for someone who is genuinely saved to "lose their salvation?" The Calvinist asserts that the warning passages of Scripture are either addressed to unbelievers who imagine that they are believers, or to actual believers in Jesus, who are "helped along the way" with such exhortations.

Logic tells us however that these verses cannot apply to unbelievers for they need no warning to not depart from the faith of which they never belonged. On the other hand, neither would those who are genuinely saved by God's irresistible grace need to be warned of falling away. Their unconditional election from the foundation of the earth makes it impossible for them to do so. They will always be preserved by God until the end without fail.

These shallow Calvinist answers will not do, for the Bible makes it clear concerning the believer's perseverance. By carefully looking at Scripture in its proper context, while not reading into each text with preconceived notions, we can see who the New Testament writers were writing about and what was their intended purpose. If we believe that all Scripture is fully inspired by God and communicated to us by the Holy Spirit for practical purposes, every warning must be in there for a specific and necessary reason [2 Timothy 3:15; 2 Peter 1:20,21].

God made sure that practically every book of the New Testament contained the warning of the reality of *falling away* from the faith.[89]

> 1 Timothy 4:1 "Now the Spirit expressly says that in latter times *some will depart from the faith*, giving heed to deceiving spirits and doctrines of demons,"
>
> 2 Thessalonians 2:3 "Let no one deceive you by any means; for that Day will not come unless *the falling away* (apostasia) comes first, and the man of sin is revealed, the son of perdition,"

To fall away in New Testament language is to commit "apostasy." The Greek word *apostasia* means to depart or turn away, implying that one is turning from something he once held fast to. Interestingly, Jesus used an almost identical word, *apostasion*, when He spoke of divorce [Matthew 5:31; 19:7; Mark 10:4]. Here Jesus uses the term to express a permanent separation in the relationship, where the covenant blessing of mutual relationship is no longer enjoyed.

The truth is that Scripture continually warns genuine believers of falling away because it is fully possible for them to do so. Our assurance of salvation is not arbitrary but based upon our *continuing in the faith*. So long as we hold fast and are *not moved away* from the hope of the gospel

---

[89] See David Pawson's work, "*Once Saved, Always Saved?*" (London: Hodder & Stoughton, 1996).

we have eternal life through Christ Jesus our Lord.

> Colossians 1:21-23 "You, who once were alienated and enemies in your mind by wicked works, yet now He has reconciled [thereby being a true believer] in the body of His flesh through death, to present you holy, and blameless, and above reproach in His sight-- *if indeed you continue in the faith*, grounded and steadfast, and are *not moved away* from the hope of the gospel which you heard, which was preached to every creature…"

> Hebrews 3:6 "Christ as a Son over His own house, whose house we are *if we hold fast the confidence* and the rejoicing of the hope *firm to the end*."

Time would fail me to tell of the numerous passages spoken to actual believers warning them of the possibility of losing their salvation. However, it will be helpful to highlight a few that Calvinists have to ignore or explain away to fit their theology of Unconditional Perseverance.

Jesus Himself did not take the eternal salvation of His disciples for granted. As branches only have life if they remain in the vine, so believers only have life if they continue in Christ [John 15:1-8]. They do not have life in themselves. They must abide, stay, remain and dwell in Him. Likewise, if they do not continue in Him through faith they can be "cast out" and "thrown into the fire." Unquestionably, Jesus is talking to "branches" that are already joined to Him and partaking of His life [John 15:8]. To make this refer to unbelievers makes no sense. Only a fool would command false converts to remain in Him if they were never in Him, to begin with.

> John 15:4-6 "*Abide in Me*, and I in you… I am the vine, you are the branches. He who abides in Me, and I in him, bears much fruit; for without Me you can do nothing. If anyone does not abide in Me, *he is cast out* as a branch and is withered; and *they*

gather them and throw them into the fire, and they are burned."

Jesus' brother James also warned of actual believers "wandering from the truth" by departing from the faith into deception and sin. His audience is "brethren" who are genuine converts. Nominal, unconverted Christians are not in view simply because they have already wandered from the truth having never truly believed it. Therefore, they do not need to be warned! On the contrary, God calls this wandering brother a "sinner" - someone who will lose eternal life, if he does not turn back from the error of his way to the path of truth.

> James 5:19-20 "*Brethren*, if anyone among you *wanders* from the truth, and someone turns him back, let him know that he who turns a sinner from the error of his way will *save a soul from death* and cover a multitude of sins."

A strikingly similar and parallel passage to this New Testament reference is found in the Old Testament, spoken by God through Ezekiel the prophet [Ezekiel 18:19-32]. God declared that if a godly man willfully chooses to turn away from the way of righteousness all of his righteous deeds will not be remembered. He has departed from the faith into sin having become unfaithful. And as a result, he shall die, thereby missing out on the life God offers both now and in the age to come [vv.23].

> Ezekiel 18:24 "But when a *righteous man turns away* from his righteousness and commits iniquity, and does according to all the abominations that the wicked man does, *shall he live?* All the righteousness which he has done shall not be remembered; *because of the unfaithfulness* of which he is guilty and the sin which he has committed, because of them he shall die."

The Apostle Peter also cautioned believers who had "escaped the pollutions of the world" having "known the way of righteousness," lest they fall back into their former life before Christ. Unbelievers, though they may attend church, have never escaped the pollutions of the world. They are still worldly even if they call themselves members. But Peter is not talking to them, but rather is warning genuine believers of the danger of turning back from the faith they once held fast to, saying it is better not to have been saved than to turn back from the way.

> 2 Peter 2:20-21 "For if, after *they have escaped* the pollutions of the world through the knowledge of the Lord and Savior Jesus Christ, they are *again entangled* in them and *overcome*, the latter end is worse for them than the beginning. For it would have been better for them not to have *known the way of righteousness*, than having known it, to *turn from the holy commandment* delivered to them."

One of the most explicit examples of the believer losing their eternal salvation is found in the Book of Revelation where Jesus warns the Church of Sardis that their names can be blotted out of the Book of Life if they do not overcome. Other verses tell us that all who are "written in the Book" are saved, and those who are not are lost [Revelation 21:27; 20:15]. Obviously, the only way to have your name erased from the Book of Life is for it initially to be there. Unbelievers who have never been born again were never written in this book and therefore their names cannot be removed.

> Revelation 3:5 "He who *overcomes* shall be clothed in white garments, and *I will not blot out his name from the Book of Life*, but I will confess his name before My Father and before His angels."

This simple verse from the lips of Jesus poses a significant problem for Calvinists who use the same "Book of Life" language to defend Unconditional Election. A favorite proof-text, edited by Reformed ESV translators, is Revelation 13:8 that speaks of those "whose names have been written in the Book of the Life… from the foundation of the world." However, the full text says, "All who dwell on the earth will worship him [Antichrist], whose names have not been written in the Book of Life of *the Lamb slain from the foundation of the world.*" Its context points to the fact that the Lamb was slain from the foundation of the world (i.e., God had preplanned the cross of Christ), not that God had determined a select few for salvation before He created the universe.

The dilemma is that if God has chosen disciples without condition before the foundation of the world, they cannot be un-elected. There would be no need for Jesus to say this to the believers in Sardis unless it was an empty threat [Revelation 3:5]. Nor would they be threatened by it if they assumed that either way their election was predetermined and not based on their repentance and overcoming. To put it another way, if you were the Church of Sardis and received a letter from Jesus threatening to blot your name from the Book of Life, but are also a Calvinist, would you not think Jesus was mad?

Without question, the most-debated passage relation to the possibility of someone being genuinely saved and falling away from the faith is found in Hebrews Chapter 6. Calvinists who hold to Unconditional Election have to affirm automatically that it is unbelievers who are being warned (*if they* fall away) to not depart from the faith. Whereas most Arminians contend that actual, saved believers are in view.

> Hebrews 6:4-6 "For it is impossible for those who were *once enlightened*, and have *tasted the heavenly gift*, and have become *partakers of the Holy Spirit*, and have *tasted the good word of God* and the *powers of the age to come*, if they fall away, to renew them again to repentance, since they crucify again for themselves the Son of God, and put Him to an open shame."

It is important to recognize that historically the Book of Hebrews was considered to be written to saved Jews who need to be reminded of the preeminence of Jesus Christ. Unsaved Jews reject Jesus and could care less about His supposed preeminence in their life. But this book was not written to them. It was written to "holy brethren" who have "partaken of the heavenly calling" and "consider Jesus as their Apostle and the High Priest of their confession" [Hebrews 3:1,6,12-14]. It was written to believers who have already laid the foundations of repentance and faith, and now need to go on to greater maturity [Hebrews 5:12-14; 6:1-3].

In this context, the Holy Spirit gives a clear warning of falling away. To make this text refer to Church-going unbelievers is preposterous and downright laughable. Unbelievers cannot be "renewed *again* to repentance" if they never repented in the first place. Repentance according to Calvinism is only possible if God caused them to be born again by Irresistible Grace and thereby "granted" to them. They cannot repent of their own accord and therefore a faithful Calvinist must affirm that verse 6 is referring to the elect (unless it is somehow referring to a secret, pseudo repentance, that Calvinists themselves don't believe in).

The Arminian does not embrace a falling away that promotes multiple experiences of regeneration each time one comes to the altar after sinning. To "fall away" in the full and final sense is not the same thing as falling into areas of sin and error. As the author of Hebrews writes, losing one's salvation is an act of the will that happens *once* to a believer when they *fully turn* from God and harden their heart against Him. Then and only then, it is impossible to be renewed again to repentance.

THE CONFIDENCE OF CONDITIONAL SECURITY

The hard truth is that the Bible plainly teaches that it is entirely possible for a genuine believer to lose their salvation once and for all. Though many Arminians have varying positions on assurance and eternal security, all agree that Biblical perseverance is not based on Calvinism's Unconditional Election. Our eternal salvation is based upon faith in Jesus Christ and Him alone. *Sola Fide* (by faith alone) is the basis of the believer's assurance and eternal security in Christ.

> 1 Peter 1:5 "[All true believers] are *kept* by the power of God *through faith* for salvation ready to be revealed in the last time."

Arminius himself affirmed the believer's perseverance by faith when he said,

> "With regard to the *certainty of salvation*, my opinion is, that it is possible for *him who believes* in Jesus Christ to be *certain and persuaded*, and, if his heart condemns him not, he is now in reality *assured*, that he is a Son of God, and stands in the grace of Jesus Christ."[90]

Arminians are often attacked on this point by Calvinists because we offer no assurance of salvation, if it can be lost in the end. Despite the numerous and blatantly untrue accusations against Arminians, we do not advocate a legalistic salvation that promotes works as our basis of confidence. Our assurance is Jesus, His faithfulness, and His promises. So long as we trust Him, follow Him, and continue to believe in His name we have eternal life [John 20:31].

Unlike Calvinism, our confidence is not in persevering in good works to somehow prove our election. In the end, there is no assurance in that view because one could never truly know if he were chosen from before the world began. Though you may seem to be elect now and maintain good works, in the end, it could be in vain, and your faith could be found false.

As Dave Hunt rightly points out (in quoting from R.T Kendall), it is no wonder that "nearly all of the Puritan 'divines' went through great doubt and despair on their deathbeds as they realized their lives did not give perfect evidence that they were elect."[91] Our confidence, our conviction, and our certainty of salvation is Jesus Christ and Him alone.

> 1 John 5:11-14 "This is the testimony: that *God has given us eternal life*, and this life is in His Son. He who has the Son has life; he who does not have the Son of God does not have life. These

---

[90] James Arminius. *The Works of James Arminius.* (Grand Rapids: Baker Book House, 1986), Vol. 2 p. 667.
[91] Dave Hunt, *What Love is This? Calvinism's Misrepresentation of God* (Bend OR, The Berean Call, 2013), p. 482.

things I have written to you who *believe* in the name of the Son of God, *that you may know that you have eternal life*, and that you may *continue to believe* in the name of the Son of God. Now this is the *confidence* that we have in Him…"

God has given us eternal life which is only found in His Son. Therefore, *we know* (have confident, unswerving conviction) that we have eternal life because we believe and continue to believe in the name of the Son of God. His promise is the confidence that we have in Him and the full and final assurance of our salvation.

"Frequently and explicitly preach the truth, though not in a controversial way.
Take care to do it in love and gentleness…
Answer [Calvinism's] objections, as occasion offers, both in public and private.
Do this with all possible sweetness both of look and of accent…
Make it a matter of constant and earnest prayer,
that God would stop the plague."

-John Wesley[92]

---

[92] John Wesley, The Essential Works of John Wesley (Uhrichsville, Oh: Barbour Publishing, 2011) Q.76. p. 921, 922.

10

CONCLUSION

TEN [EXTRA] REASONS TO REJECT CALVINISM

Reformed theology encompasses much more than TULIP. It affects the way we think about God, our attitudes toward man, the way we approach Scripture as a whole, our methodology for ministry, our Christology (the study of Jesus Christ), soteriology (the study of salvation), pneumatology (the study of the Holy Spirit), eschatology (the study of the last things), and every other "ology" that has to do with the Christian faith.

Understand that when one signs up for Calvinism they are taking on much more than the doctrines of TULIP. They are taking on the entire framework of Reformed, Covenant theology that brings with it many other damaging theological beliefs in its wake. To be sure, each of these points does not apply to every Calvinist or every Reformed-leaning ministry. Instead, these "ten [extra] reasons" to reject Calvinism are personal observations that are common among those who embrace Reformed theology.

1. Calvinism has the potential to breed spiritual pride.

At the heart of Five-Point Calvinism is often a spiritual pride that sees others as second-class Christians. Anyone who is non-Calvinist is accused of being intellectually challenged, man-centered, works-focused and humanistic in their thinking. They might be Christians, but they are inferior Christians. That is if these dubious believers have ever been born again in the first place. As one famous Calvinist teacher says, "I believe that Arminians *may* be born-again Christians."[93] The implication is that most non-Calvinists are not saved because they have believed in an inferior gospel.

Seeking to critique or disprove of anyone's salvation experience, except for the express purpose of evangelism enflames pride in the human heart. We begin to look down upon others, show them little respect, develop a critical spirit, and become unteachable when it comes to others who are not as reformed in their faith. Never forget that God hates spiritual pride [Proverbs 6:16,17]. Everyone proud in heart is an abomination to the Lord [Proverbs 16:5]. And therefore, no matter how much one understands the glory of God, God will continue to resist those that are proud and show grace to the humble [1 Peter 5:5].

2. *Calvinism tends to exalt theology over God.*

One of the dangers inherent within Calvinism is the tendency to exalt theology and doctrine over God Himself. Sound teaching is critically important and necessary, yet it is possible to turn theology into an idol that we worship in place of God. When our Christian mission in life becomes more about proving the sovereignty of God than loving Jesus with all of our heart, we have missed the Spirit of God and stepped into error. Our central purpose in life is not to preach Calvinism or Arminianism, but Jesus Christ and Him crucified [1 Corinthians 2:2].

Don't get me wrong. I love theology. One of my favorite books of all time is Grudem's Systematic Theology. But hang around a staunch Calvinist long enough, and you will find that many are more concerned about proving Calvinism than they are about winning souls and equipping the Church to walk in wholeheartedness before the Lord. Be careful not to fall into the trap of searching the Scriptures so that you can prove your doctrines when all along it was meant to lead you to Jesus Christ in love and intimacy [John 5:39,40].

---

[93] Edwin H. Palmer, *The Five Points of Calvinism* (Grand Rapids: Baker Book House, 1980), p. 26.

3. *Calvinism can hinder men from intimacy with God.*

The God spoken of by Calvinists is big, powerful, omnipotent and glorious. One thing I admire about Calvinism is that it loathes the namby-pamby God often trumpeted by modern evangelicalism. However, within the camp of Reformed theology, one has to guard against constructing a God who is stoic, distant, emotionless, and detached from personal fellowship with man. Yes, God is glorious and sovereign, but He is also intimately involved in the everyday lives of weak men and women like you and me.

Calvinists themselves acknowledge that their theology takes faith, repentance and free will away from man and places them entirely upon God so that He gets all of the glory. It sounds noble until one understands that it turns men into mere robots and hinders voluntary love and intimacy with Him. Coerced Calvinism flies in the face of God's design for relationship with man. God created us that we might receive His love and freely give it back to Him as an act of our will. This purpose is why we were made. God made us for Himself with the express purpose of giving Him our voluntary love forever.

4. *Calvinism can significantly hinder persistent prayer.*

Calvinism, if fully believed and consistently practiced, hinders persistent, faith-filled prayer. By embracing a hyper view of God's sovereignty, one is led to conclude that our prayers ultimately do not matter because God's sovereign will is always done. No matter how much we may say otherwise, and no matter how much a Calvinist would call men to pray, their doctrine works directly against them and quenches the Spirit of Prayer. If God's will is always done regardless of anything man does, prayer does not truly matter.

I am not saying that Calvinists do not pray, but that persistent prayer which lays hold of God's promises and labors for the souls of men is counter to Calvinism itself. If God has decreed from eternity who will be saved and who will be damned, nothing can stop, aid, or hinder His sovereign plan! We can sit at ease and cease from praying for men's souls. If Calvinism is true, let us close our Church and homes to prayer and wait for God's perfect will to be accomplished.

5. *Calvinism, if put into practice, will obstruct evangelism.*

Nothing is more detrimental to evangelism than Calvinism's claim that God has already decided who will be saved, and there is nothing more that we can do to change it. A true Calvinist cannot stand in front of a crowd of ten thousand and say with the Apostle Paul that God calls all men everywhere to repent that they might be saved. Calvinism says that God does not call all men to repent and believe but only those already chosen and pre-programmed to do so. A God who only sent His Son to die for the elect (with no others in mind) would not offer salvation to all men.

In the parable of the Talents, Jesus rebuked the man with one talent because he made a grave mistake regarding God's sovereignty. His excuse for laziness was rooted in one statement: "Lord, I knew you to be a hard man, *reaping where you have not sown, and gathering where you have not scattered seed*" [Matthew 25:24]. In addition to misunderstanding the nature of God, this man joined the camp of hyper-sovereignty because he knew that the master "reaps even where one has not sown" and "gathers even where one has not scattered seed." His false conclusion rooted in a wrong view of sovereignty said, "What does it matter what I do? Either way, you're going to get the harvest." Concerning evangelism, this is the quintessential danger of Calvinism. It lessens man's responsibility and promotes laziness in personal soul winning.

6. *Calvinism often promotes unbelief and quenches the gifts of the Holy Spirit.*

As a Charismatic pastor, I have witnessed firsthand how Calvinism's theology of God's sovereignty has quenched the ministry and gifts of the Holy Spirit on both a personal and corporate level. The most significant hindrance to the Holy Spirit's ministry in all of its facets is unbelief. All gifts of the Holy Spirit function by faith [Acts 3:16; Romans 12:6; James 5:15]. There is a certain level of risk and uncertainty in stepping out which is why all things, including prophecy, must be tested with Scripture [1 Thessalonians 5:19-21]. When we pray for healing or operate in spiritual gifts, we trust and believe God to move, but we are not always sure of its manifestation.

When the sovereignty of God is taken to extremes, one cannot help but think that God Himself not only allows, but puts all sickness and disease on people to teach them a lesson. When we begin to blame every sore throat on God, we have no grounds to believe Him to heal the very thing He wants us to have. God does *use* sickness and suffering, and can teach us through it. However, never in Scripture are they *ordained* by Him as a primary means of discipleship or sanctification. If that be the case, we would all be sick, all the time, in the worst way, because we all are significantly in need of more Christ-likeness.

7. *Calvinism usually teaches a non-literal interpretation of Bible Prophecy.*

Augustine's intense spiritualizing of Scripture has been passed down to those in the Reformed camp by the droves. While the Book of Romans is exegeted to its depths, the Old Testament Prophets such as Isaiah, Ezekiel, and Jeremiah are spiritualized away. Any Christian should know that spiritualizing prophetic passages of Scripture is a dangerous method of interpretation. When one spiritualizes God's Word the interpreter becomes the final authority instead of Scripture. More than not it leads believers down the road of deception and unbiblical error.

The Bible is an infallible book of prophecies. Before Christ came to the earth the first time, there were hundreds of Old Testament prophecies that foretold His coming. It is interesting to note that every one of these predictions was fulfilled at face value, which was Matthew's express purpose for writing his gospel. He was proving that Christ is the *literal fulfillment* of prophecy. Because of this, we can safely assume that all prophecy was meant to be understood literally. God means what He says and says what He means unless the context itself proves that it is symbolic.

8. *Calvinism typically promotes Preterism.*

Because of a non-literal interpretation of Scripture, many within the Reformed camp have encouraged Preterism. Behind Preterism is the unbiblical idea that most prophecies concerning Christ's second coming were already fulfilled in 70 A.D. Preterists argue that the Olivet Discourse and the Book of Revelation have no future fulfillment and claim that all End-Time prophecies which speak of the great tribulation, antichrist, and second coming of Jesus were fulfilled when Jerusalem was destroyed by Rome. Without question, the Book of Revelation has always had relevance to all Christians since the First Century, reminding believers that God's plan to triumph over His enemies will not be thwarted. And it can be argued that some of the events of Matthew 24 have been partially fulfilled.

However, Nero was not the Antichrist. The Great Tribulation has not yet happened. Jesus' return "in the clouds" did not occur in 70 A.D. The gathering of the elect has not taken place. And God has not replaced Israel with the Church. The arguments against Preterism are more than can be numbered, but here are just a few: The Book of Revelation says that Jesus will come so that every eye sees Him [1:7], Jerusalem will be trodden down by the Gentiles for 42 months [11:1,2], the two witnesses will prophesy 1,260 days then be killed 3 ½ days later and rise from the dead [11:3-12], every person on the earth will be required to take a mark in order to buy and sell [13:16-18], and the Euphrates River will dry up to make way for the kings of the east to gather for the great battle [16:12]; all of which have never happened in 70 A.D, nor ever have occurred in history.

9. *Calvinism breeds Replacement Theology and the neglect of God's purpose for Israel.*

Reformed, Covenant Theology claims that God's relationship with man is divided into two covenants- the Covenant of Works and the Covenant of Grace. Dispensationalism, on the other hand, focuses on the specific covenants mentioned in the Bible such as the Abrahamic Covenant, the Mosaic Covenant, the Davidic Covenant, and the New Covenant. Unlike Dispensationalism, Covenant Theology does not embrace a clear distinction between Israel and the Church but instead sees them as one people of God- Israel in the Old Testament, the Church in the New.

Multitudes of Reformed theologians believe that the Church is now Israel. Since the cross, the Church has become the sole recipient of Israel's Old Testament prophetic promises and in that sense, we have "replaced Israel" and inherited their blessings. They also claim that Israel has forfeited their place as God's people because of unbelief, and now God has moved His attention to the Church. This subtle form of Replacement Theology has led Calvinists to discredit God's plan for Israel's restoration and "boast against the natural branches," something that Paul warns as being serious before God lest we too are cut off by Him [Romans 11:17-22, 25-26, 29; Jeremiah 31:31-37; Acts 15:15-16]. May we all take to heart the words of Spurgeon himself, who said,

> "I think we do not attach sufficient importance to *the restoration of the Jews*. We do not think enough of it. But certainly, if there is anything promised in the Bible it is this. I imagine that you cannot read the Bible without seeing clearly that *there is to be an actual restoration of the children of Israel*...May that happy day soon come!"[94]

10. Calvinism embraces wrong views of the Coming Kingdom and Millennial Reign of Jesus.

Reformed Theology has no single eschatological view; however chief among its beliefs concerning the second coming of Christ and His

---

[94] Charles H. Spurgeon, *The C. H. Spurgeon Collection, Metropolitan Tabernacle Pulpit*, I, no. 28, 1855 (Albany, Oregon: Ages Software, 1998), p. 382.

kingdom are Amillennialism and Postmillennialism, which come from Origen and Augustine's allegorical way of interpretation and spiritual concept of the Kingdom. Both views deny a literal reign of Christ upon the earth after the second coming and teach a present, spiritual reign of Christ that strictly happens now invisibly within our hearts. The only difference is that Postmillennialism is more optimistic in believing that the Church will convert the world and fully usher in the Kingdom over all the earth before Jesus returns.

Both beliefs claim that Revelation 20 is not to be taken literally, but applied spiritually to the Church throughout history. Thus, the "thousand years" is symbolic, Satan is already "bound" and no longer able to "deceive the nations," and the Church is now "reigning on the earth." This Greek mindset is contrary to the Hebrew understanding of reigning with the Messiah on the earth in a literal way. Six times John repeats the phrase "a thousand years" thereby making it next to impossible to spiritualize away [Revelation 20:2,3,4,5,6,7]. Jesus will return and reign with His saints for a thousand years and fulfill His covenant promises to Israel. As Calvinist J.C. Ryle said,

> "Reader, however great the difficulties surrounding many parts of unfulfilled prophecy, two points appear to my own mind to stand out as plainly as if written by a sunbeam. One of these points is *the second personal advent of our Lord Jesus Christ before the Millennium.* The other of these events is the *future literal gathering of the Jewish nation, and their restoration to their own land.* I tell no man that these two truths are essential to salvation, and that he cannot be saved except he sees them with my eyes. But I tell any man that these truths appear to me distinctly set down in holy Scripture and that the denial of them is as astonishing and incomprehensible to my own mind as the denial of the divinity of Christ."[95]

---

[95] J. C. Ryle, *Are You Ready For The End Of Time?* (Fearn, Scotland: Christian Focus, 2001) p. 112-115; reprint of *Coming Events and Present Duties.*

A FINAL WORD

If you have read this far, it should be no surprise to you that I am fully persuaded Calvinism is a dangerous theology that should be rejected. The Five Points of TULIP and Covenant Theology as a whole are riddled with error concerning God, His nature, and His plan of salvation. When we put on the lens of Reformed Theology, our entire belief system becomes distorted and disfigured in a way that God never intended for the believer. We begin to see God's Word in a different light, and I dare say *wrong* light that breeds spiritual pride and confusion.

I know that may seem bold to some Arminians and offensive to most Calvinists, but I am utterly persuaded it is true. I have read book after book from many of the Calvinist greats and have carefully read and prayed through their pages with a Bible in hand and an open mind. Through it, I have come to the conclusion that *Calvinism, firmly believed and persistently practiced, is a major hindrance to true Apostolic Christianity.*

My purpose in writing *Unchosen* was to expose some of the blatant errors and inconsistencies that come with Calvinism's Five Points of theology. I have written this book for all believers- Charismatic and non-Charismatic, Evangelical and Pentecostal, Reformed and non-Reformed – to show that TULIP with all of its petals should be uprooted and abandoned as being the "only true gospel" of Scripture.

The gospel is the good news of Jesus Christ and what He has accomplished in redeeming man from sin. It displays His incredible plan to restore man back to a place of intimate relationship with Him forever. It is good news indeed! But the Gospel of Calvinism is not good news for the planet. It is only good news for the elect who are lucky enough to be chosen for salvation and not damned by God's eternal decree.

To the rest of humanity, who are left unchosen, we ought to say, "Good luck with your life as you store up God's anger and wrath for the Day of Judgment. God has not chosen you because He cares more about His glory than your good. He loves you enough to give you temporal, earthly benefits; but not enough to give you eternal life. Heaven was never your home. You were predestined or hell from the foundations of the earth. Sorry about your luck… but you were never chosen!"

If however the Bible is true, that God fully loves everyone in the world [John 3:16], and truly desires all men to be saved [1 Timothy 2:3,4], so much so that He sent forth His Son to be the propitiation for all the world [1 John 2:2], that perhaps all through Him might believe [John 1:7]; then let us reject TULIP and weed it from our theological garden. Let us go forth with the good news to every creature under heaven crying out with the Spirit until Jesus returns,

> "Come! Let *him who hears*, Come! Let *him who thirsts*, Come! *Whoever desires*, let him take of the water of life freely!" [Revelation 22:17]

ABOUT THE AUTHOR

Tyler Miller is the Senior Pastor of Preaching and Prayer at the Upper Room in York, PA. He is married to Alexandra and has two children, Eden and Wesley. Tyler is passionate about calling the Church to prayer and power evangelism, preparing believers for the Second Coming of Jesus, and seeing the fullness of the Holy Spirit transforms lives.

To contact the author about speaking at your church or conference, please visit www.upperroomyork.com or Isaiah403.org.

Made in the USA
Columbia, SC
30 December 2017